GREY EMINENCE

FOX CONNER AND THE ART OF MENTORSHIP

By Edward Cox

Foreword by
Lieutenant General David H. Huntoon, Jr.

NEW
FORUMS
Stillwater, Oklahoma
U.S.A.

NEW FORUMS PRESS INC.

Published in the United States of America
by New Forums Press, Inc.1018 S. Lewis St.
Stillwater, OK 74074
www.newforums.com

Portions of this book were previously published online as
Edward Cox, *Grey Eminence: Fox Conner and the Art of Mentorship*,
Land Warfare Paper 78W (Arlington, Va.: Association of the United
Sates Army, September 2010). Used with permission.

Library of Congress Cataloging-in-Publication Data Pending

This book may be ordered in bulk quantities at discount from New
Forums Press, Inc., P.O. Box 876, Stillwater, OK 74076 [Federal I.D.
No. 73 1123239]. Printed in the United States of America.

ISBN 10: 1-58107-203-1

ISBN 13: 978-1-581072-03-7

Contents

Foreword

Major Ed Cox's biography of Major General Fox Conner offers a rare opportunity to examine the life of a remarkable military leader and teacher. Fox Conner graduated from the United States Military Academy in the spring of 1898, and served our country in uniform for four decades. He was General Pershing's "indispensable man" during World War I, and a guiding force behind the success of Generals Marshall, Eisenhower, and Patton. He was a consummate professional soldier and master mentor.

At West Point, Fox Conner graduated in the middle of his class and earned more than his fair share of demerits. The story of his transformation into a lifelong learner who became the Army's foremost expert on field artillery doctrine, while teaching himself French, Spanish, and German along the way – is an inspiration to all aspiring leaders. Conner's model of mentoring junior officers also provides an excellent example for all leaders to emulate.

Fox Conner introduced the tank to Patton, inspired Eisenhower to become a student of military history and strategy, and contributed to the expertise that George C. Marshall employed in organizing allied commands. Conner's life represents the epitome of the professional officer and is a model for today's Army officer and for all leaders.

Before Conner became an exceptional teacher, he was a dedicated and disciplined learner. He became the Army's expert on artillery by studying with the experts – the French Army. He learned how to make American artillery pieces fire faster, more accurately and more efficiently during his time as an exchange officer with a French artillery regiment.

In the first two decades of the twentieth century, Europeans wrote far more about the study of war than Americans. Conner's French and Spanish language skills allowed him the opportunity to study those texts not yet translated into English. He taught himself German as a captain in order to read the latest publications on strategy from the Prussian *Kriegsakademie.*

Some of Fox Conner's career developmental experiences are similar to those West Point uses today to build leaders of character. Just as Fox Conner studied abroad to learn a different culture and to establish allied relationships, so do Cadets, many of whom spend a semester abroad. Just as Fox Conner was fluent in foreign languages, there are foreign language requirements for every Cadet at West Point. Fox Conner knew that one of the key traits of a professional is a habit of lifelong learning. Cadets begin that journey by developing a depth of knowledge in one of 45 different major areas of study during their time at the Academy. Their instructors serve as exemplars of the profession, modeling habits of intellectual curiosity and mentoring cadets, both inside the classroom and out, and inspiring them to develop knowledge across a wide range of subjects.

As I write this foreword, the U.S. Army has entered its tenth year of combat in Afghanistan. Tens of thousands of Soldiers, sailors, airmen and Marines are deployed around the globe in support of U.S. national interests. Our Army has tremendous resources in terms of weapons, power-projection capabilities, and technology, but our most important resource is people. As professionals, each of us has an obligation to identify and develop talents within our subordinates to ensure our collective ability to provide for the Nation's defense. Each of us is engaged in leader development and a commitment to lifelong learning.

Ed Cox's book is both a tribute to one man's extraordinary impact on the U.S. Army, and a study in how to develop an organization's strategic leaders through mentorship. Leaders at every level will learn much from this book about the exemplary life of Major General Fox Conner.

Lieutenant General David H. Huntoon, Jr.
December 2010

Acknowledgements

A project of this magnitude generates a long list of people to whom I owe a debt of gratitude. First, I'd like to thank the librarians and curators who have patiently answered my questions and tracked down obscure resources for me. I'm grateful to the Calhoun County Historical and Genealogical Society of Pittsboro, Mississippi, especially Larry Hellums, who was very helpful and encouraging. I'd like to thank the Casemate Museum, the Ordnance Association, and the George Casey Memorial Library at Fort Hood, Texas.

I owe a special debt of thanks to the staffs of the United States Military Academy Library, the Library of Congress, the Eisenhower Library, and the George C. Marshall Foundation. I am also indebted to Norm Macdonald and the Ossining Historical Society in Ossining, New York, and to Jerry Parker, who selflessly shared his insights and sources about Fox Conner. I wish to thank Robert Citino for his advice, encouragement, and editorial contributions, and to Sandra Daugherty at the Association of the United States Army.

Thank you to the staff and faculty of the Social Sciences and History Departments at West Point for encouraging and enabling me to complete this work, especially Colonels Michael Meese, Cindy Jebb, Matthew Moten, Gian Gentile, and Jeffrey Peterson; Lieutenant Colonel Tania Chacho, Majors Matt Lennox and Faith

Chamberlain, Dr. James Forest, Dr. Thom Sherlock, Dr. Ben Mitchell, and Dr. Scott Silverstone. I owe particular thanks to Colonel Isaiah Wilson and Dr. Don Snider, two men for whom I have the highest regard and I'm proud to call them mentors. Thanks to my peers and colleagues in the Sosh Department for tolerating my passion for this subject.

Last and most significantly, I wish to thank my wife Ellyn, who is the love of my life. It has been almost a decade since I remarked in a casual way that someone ought to write the story of MG Fox Conner, and that I was going to be the man to do it. Her encouragement of my endeavor has never waned, even to the point of allowing me to plan family vacations to coincide with my research. Thank you for continuing to love me as I love and serve my country.

Edward Cox
January 2011

INTRODUCTION

October, 1913
Fort Riley, Kansas

Captain Fox Conner and his wife Virginia settled into their seats. Their train slowly pulled away from the station in Kansas City, gaining speed as it rolled across the plains towards Fort Riley, Kansas. The Conners were returning to the Army post following their annual trek to visit Virginia's family in the Adirondack mountains of New York. As they sat in the gently rocking passenger car, Fox and his wife noticed a young Army officer seated at the other end of the car. The man's appearance fascinated Mrs. Conner. Eyes front, the young officer sat erect, swaying with the motion of the clattering car, holding the largest cavalry saber she had ever seen. In all the time she watched his stern face, it never changed expression. Fox also had been intently eyeing the man, and halfway to Fort Riley he walked down the train car aisle and introduced himself to George Patton.[1]

Though only a lieutenant, Patton was already a celebrity within the Army. He was the only American officer to compete in the 1912 Olympics in Sweden, finishing fifth in the modern pentathlon. While stationed at Fort Myer, Virginia, Patton had published articles about his profession and attracted the attention and patronage of important officials like Secretary of War Henry Stimson and Major General Leonard Wood, the Army chief of staff.

While Conner was returning to Riley, Patton was reporting there for the first time to attend the Mounted Service School, having spent six weeks in France at his own expense studying swordsmanship.[2] As they talked on the train, they discovered that they had many interests in common, the most important being the Army, horses, family and their country. This chance meeting blossomed into friendship, and as the years passed they discovered a shared ardor for hunting and fishing. More than once Beatrice Patton and Virginia Conner joined them in their adventures on the deep blue waters off the Straits of Florida and the Caribbean, as well as North American lakes and streams.

In Patton, the older Conner found a compatible, ambitious young man who shared his regard for history, literature, and knowledge in general. As a child, Patton had suffered from dyslexia, but his family had compensated for his reading disability with intense exercises of oral lessons and reading aloud to him. As a result, Patton had developed the habits of an earnest listener. He recognized in Conner a master strategist and eagerly sought his advice and counsel. Conner in turn was a willing and able teacher who transformed lectures into conversations of equals. Most importantly, Conner was the first man who tried to interest Patton in a new war machine called a "tank."

July, 1918
Chaumont, France

The sun had already set when George C. Marshall reported to his new assignment at General Pershing's headquarters in Chaumont. This bustling city with a population of 20,000 lay in the upper Marne region of France. Chaumont was a relatively young town by European standards, being only one thousand years old. It's location in the scenic rolling countryside between what were once the feudal kingdoms of Burgundy and Lorraine.[3] By selecting Chaumont as the location for the American Expeditionary Forces' General Headquarters, or AEF GHQ, Pershing took advantage of the town's strategic railroad station.[4]

The GHQ occupied a four-story barracks building which was formerly the home of a French regiment.[5] Marshall ascended the stairs to the second floor of the main barrack building and entered the hub of the AEF, a small room measuring 18 feet by 12 feet. A map of the western front dominated one wall. A lone desk sat in the middle of the room, where General John "Black Jack" Pershing would sit to receive updates from his staff.[6] The AEF was growing by thousands of soldiers each day and would swell to over a million men over the next year as the Americans helped their allies to smash the German army. For now, however, George Marshall would not report directly to Pershing but instead to his chief of operations, Colonel Fox Conner.

Marshall had attracted Conner's attention while serving as the operations officer for the 1st American Division seven months earlier. Conner believed in walking the ground rather than relying on reports sent back to Chaumont from the division headquarters. It was through one of these observation trips that he heard about Marshall from Major Robert Lewis, a liaison officer to the French Army.[7] Conner arranged to meet Marshall and was very impressed. A busy man himself, Conner began devoting one day each week to working with Marshall at the 1st Division headquarters in Menil-la-Tour.[8] It was not long before Conner reached down from Chaumont and plucked Marshall to work in his section.

Together they planned the strategies for what would be the decisive battles of the Great War, and forged a friendship that would last until Conner's death in 1951. Marshall would go on to become Chief of Staff of the Army during World War II, Secretary of Defense, and Secretary of State. The plan he devised for rebuilding Europe in the 1950s would influence American foreign policy for decades. Even after all of his successes, Marshall would maintain that he owed his greatest debts to the lessons he learned from Fox Conner.

October, 1920
Fort Meade, Maryland

One brisk fall weekend, George Patton found himself escorting his old friend and mentor as he inspected the Infantry Tank School at Fort Meade, Maryland. Brigadier General Fox Conner was serving as the Chief of Staff to General Pershing in Washington, DC, and had recently helped Pershing prepare his Congressional testimony regarding the National Defense Act, which had passed into law four months earlier. Patton had served in Pershing's headquarters at Chaumont and had known Conner since their days at Fort Riley seven years earlier.

As the men toured the grounds of Fort Meade, Conner's wife Virginia caught up with Beatrice Patton. The men rejoined them for coffee and Conner mentioned that he was due to take over command of Camp Gaillard in Panama. He was looking for a capable young officer to serve as his executive officer. His time on the Army staff during and after the war had left him out of touch with young officers, so he asked Patton for a recommendation. Only one name came to Patton's mind, that of his good friend and next door neighbor, Major Dwight David Eisenhower.[9]

Intrigued, Conner asked to meet Major Eisenhower, who was known to all of his friends as Ike. Patton obliged and arranged a dinner at his home the following afternoon. Conner made no mention of the position in Panama as the three couples ate that

Sunday but found the young major very impressive. The fact that Patton recommended him carried great weight with Conner, and a few weeks later a formal offer to Ike arrived in the mail. Thus began the most professionally enriching relationship of Ike's life. His time in Panama under Conner's tutelage would revive an interest in military history, help him to deal with the grief of his recently deceased son Icky, and prepare him for his eventual role as the Supreme Allied Commander, Europe, during World War II. Ike would go on to become President of the United States in 1952 and meet distinguished leaders from all over the world, but he would often describe Fox Conner as "the ablest man I ever knew."[10]

Finding Fox Conner

This book chronicles the untold story of one of the greatest military minds of the twentieth century and how his influence helped to put in place the great generals who won World War II. It is a book about friendship, professionalism, mentorship, and selfless devotion to country. Most of all though, this is a book about officership.

The study of officership is the study of leadership. Like all professions, the two-fold mission of the officer corps is to develop expert knowledge and to impart that knowledge to future generations. The debate about how to do this imparting resurfaces periodically throughout our nation's history, and it is a hot topic today with an army struggling to transform while facing massive mid-career officer shortages and fighting two counterinsurgencies. In studying the art of leadership, we would do well to recall one of the master mentors of the Army, Major General Fox Conner.

To those who have heard of him, Fox Conner's name is synonymous with mentorship. He is the "grey eminence" within the Army whose influence helped to shape the careers of George Patton, George Marshall, and, most notably, President Dwight Eisenhower. Hailed by his peers, subordinates and superiors as a consummate master of the art of war, Conner was a respected practitioner of his craft for four decades, but little is known about Fox Conner himself.

In military history, Conner's name is usually invoked in anecdotes about his relationship with Eisenhower, his most famous protégé, but these anecdotes do not give us the full measure of the man. What motivated Conner to develop such a masterful grasp of Army organization, strategy, and command, qualities that made him invaluable to Pershing as his chief operations officer? Why did he choose to continue to serve in the Army after the Great War, an Army shackled with budget cuts and constrained by a public that longed for isolation? With his wife's personal wealth and his close friendship with Pershing, Conner could have easily left the Army after World War I and lived a quiet life of comfort. Instead, he continued to serve for another two decades in uniform, mentoring countless young officers who would grow to be the battlefield and strategic leaders of the military during World War II. A study of his life and his method for identifying talented subordinates and developing them for future strategic leadership positions offers contemporary readers a highly salient example to emulate.

The dearth of information about Conner is not accidental. After a career that spanned four decades, this master strategist ordered all of his papers and journals burned. Because of this, most of what is known about Conner is oblique, as a passing reference in the memoirs of other great men. This book combines existing scholarship with long-forgotten references and unpublished original sources to achieve a more comprehensive picture of this dedicated public servant. The portrait that emerges provides a model for developing strategic leaders that still holds true today. Though it sounds too simple to be true, Conner continued to serve because he loved being a soldier. He was in the room when the Treaty of Versailles was signed, ending World War I. He saw in that imperfect document the beginnings of another global conflict, and he dedicated the next twenty years to training the officers who would lead American troops in battle when the clarion sounded once more. Conner was a master of his craft who recognized and recruited talented subordinates. He encouraged and challenged his protégés to develop their strengths and overcome their weaknesses, and he wasn't afraid to break rules to do it.

Master of His Craft

In 1894, Fox Conner entered the United States Military Academy upon the recommendation of Mississippi Congressman Hernando De Soto Money. Favoritism in Academy appointments was not uncommon in those days, and Fox may have benefited from this practice. His uncle, Fuller Fox, was a friend of Congressman Money and an active member of the Democratic Party. Although the U.S. Army was not an esteemed occupation in the late 1800s, West Point was the preferred avenue of entry for those with a military temperament.

The son of a Civil War sharpshooter who lost his sight at the Battle of Atlanta, Fox grew up listening to war stories and had dreamed of attending West Point since he was eight years old. Both of Fox's parents taught in the local school, and he delayed his entry at West Point for a year to prepare for the rigorous academics there. Despite this, Fox was no more than an average cadet. When he graduated from West Point in 1898, he was 17th in a class of 59 and had earned 384 demerits along the way, mostly for smoking and tardiness.

Through persistent self-study, often stretching into the evening hours, this average cadet transformed himself in the two decades following his graduation to become the foremost authority in the Army on artillery doctrine and the cornerstone of General Pershing's staff in Chaumont during World War I. This man, who consistently ranked in the bottom half of his class in foreign languages at West Point, taught himself French, German, and Spanish and served as the first American exchange officer to a French artillery unit in 1911. He would put his language skills to use again seven years later, serving as Pershing's interpreter during the Armistice negotiations. He was one of only three officers to skip the first year of the Army's two year General Service and Staff College because of his proficiency in tactics. Instead he served as an instructor, training colonels though he was only a captain at the time.

At the outbreak of World War I, Fox Conner played a pivotal role as the chief of the Operations Section of the American Expeditionary Forces under General John J. "Black Jack" Pershing, a position that didn't exist until Conner created it. Indeed, his organization of the AEF staff remains the model followed by American units to this day. Conner oversaw the planning for the Saint-Mihiel salient and the Meuse-Argonne offensive, two of the pivotal battles of the war. After the war, he wrote the official after-action report of AEF operations. He served as Pershing's chief of staff and helped him to prepare to testify before Congressional military committees. Through these assignments, he had influence over the National Defense Act of 1920. Pershing would later say to Conner, "I could have spared any other man in the A.E.F. better than you."

Recognize Talent and Develop It

Marshall, Patton, and Eisenhower are names familiar to every student of American history. Each played a key role in the American military during World War II and left their mark on the military and the country for decades. Each of these three luminaries attributed a great deal of their success in their military careers to their relationship with Fox Conner. This is not to say that he is the sole reason for their success. Indeed, each was a formidable leader in his own right before working for Conner, and each had other sponsors and patrons who facilitated their rise toward the Army's highest ranks. Conner gave each of them two things.

His first contribution, and what each recognized as memorable and lasting, was the opportunity to hone their talents under the supervision of a master strategist who became a friend and father figure. Conner recognized the talents of each one of these officers and recruited them to work for him. He summoned Marshall to his operations section in Pershing's Chaumont headquarters, eventually delegating most of the planning responsibility for the Saint-Mihiel salient to him. He travelled widely during the war with Patton, and often met with Patton to encourage him in his interest in armored vehicles. Impressed with Eisenhower after meeting him at a dinner party the Patton's hosted, he invited Ike to be his executive officer in Panama. The daily operations orders Ike had to write for Conner in Panama gave him the training he needed to graduate first in his class at Leavenworth in 1926. Conner supported Patton's development of armor doctrine in the interwar period and even endorsed a machine gun mount that Patton had invented for procurement by the Army. Throughout their careers until his retirement, each of these three junior officers would find their paths crossing with their mentor.

Conner retired to his hunting lodge in 1938 before the start of World War II, but each of these three generals wrote to him for advice throughout the war. It was not uncommon for classified couriers to travel the eight miles from the railroad to Conner's cabin near Brandreth, New York with satchels full of war plans for him to peruse and comment on. They so valued his opinion that he was consulted on operations ranging from the North Africa campaign to the invasion of Normandy.

Be Prepared to Break the Rules

Conner's second contribution to each of these famous men is more contentious. At pivotal moments in their lives, when the future held either continued success or obscurity, Fox Conner was there to provide advice, lend assistance, or call in a favor. In today's egalitarian Army, this point causes perhaps the most discomfort. Conner was not afraid to call in favors. He did not hesitate to bend or even break the rules for his protégés if he thought the circumstances warranted it. When Ike could not get released from Camp Meade because he was the post football team's coach, Conner intervened. He put in a call to Pershing to ensure Ike received orders to Panama. Later, he called in a favor with a classmate to make sure Ike attended Command and General Staff College at Leavenworth over the explicit objections of the two-star general in charge of Ike's branch. Conner rescued Patton's career with a well-timed evaluation as his senior rater while commanding the Hawaiian Division. He wasn't afraid to ask his protégés for favors either, as he did after retirement when he requested special treatment from Marshall for Trimble Brown, a former aide-de-camp.

This is favoritism in its purest form, but those who criticize this aspect of mentorship would do well to look at the results before passing final judgment. If Conner is guilty of anything, it is that he was willing to act on their behalf at crucial points in their careers to make sure they were afforded every opportunity to excel. Eisenhower put it best in his memoirs.

> To the cynic, all this may seem proof of "It's not what you know, it's who you know." There is just enough truth in that phrase to assure its survival so long as humans must save face or nurse an ego. . . . Always try to associate yourself closely with and learn as much as you can from those who know more than you, who do better than you, who see more clearly than you. . . Apart from the rewards of friendship, the association might pay off at some unforeseen time – that is only an accidental by-product. The important thing is that the learning will make you a better person.[11]

The record of Conner's disciples speaks for itself. Eisenhower went on to become Supreme Allied Commander and President of the United States, but always maintained that Conner was the person who most shaped his career. Marshall became Chief of Staff of the Army, Secretary of Defense, and Secretary of State, but maintained that he owed his greatest debts to Conner. Patton lives on in infamy as one of the greatest battlefield commanders in American history, but his talents, by his own admission, paled in comparison to Conner's grasp of the art of war. The Conner model leader development holds true today, and it is time for his story to be told.

Notes

[1] Dorothy Brandon, *Mamie Doud Eisenhower, A Portrait of a First Lady.* New York: Scribner's, 1954, 122.

[2] Carlo D'Este, *Patton: A Genius for War.* New York: Harper Collins, 1996, 140.

[3] James Harbord, *Leaves from a War Diary.* New York: Dodd, Mead, 1925, 139.

[4] Harbord, 163.

[5] Edward Coffman, *The War to End All Wars.* New York: Oxford University Press, 1968, 131.

[6] Ibid., 131.

[7] Robert Payne, *The Marshall Story.* New York: Prentice-Hall, 1951, 69.

[8] William Frye, *Marshall: Citizen Soldier.* New York: Bobbs-Merrill, 1947, 147-148.

[9] Brandon, 123.

[10] Stephen Ambrose, *Eisenhower.* Vol 1, New York: Simon and Schuster, 1984, 73.

[11] Dwight Eisenhower, *At Ease: Stories I Tell to Friends.* Garden City, NY: Doubleday, 1967, 200-201.

Chapter One
Warrior Apprentice

Son of a Soldier

Fox Conner was born on November 2, 1874, in Slate Spring, Mississippi, to Robert H. Conner and Nancy "Nannie" Fox. Both of his parents came from prominent South Carolina families who had served in the Revolutionary war.[1] In the century that followed, each family migrated from South Carolina to Alabama and eventually to Mississippi, where their paths would cross in the marriage of Robert and Nannie. By this time the fortunes of both Fox and Conner families were considerably diminished, but each held on to a family tradition that romantically emphasized their former glory.

Nannie Fox was seventeen in 1861 when her older brother Jesse joined Captain James Du Berry's Company of Mississippi Volunteers and went off to fight for the Confederacy. Robert Conner, a fellow native of Calhoun County, Mississippi, fought alongside Jesse. Robert was wounded at the Battle of Shiloh, and after his recovery he fought at Chickamauga and was wounded again. Neither of these wounds was severe, but in the Battle of Atlanta in 1864 he lost his eyesight and was discharged from the Confederate army.[2]

Despite his blindness, Bob Conner was determined to live a normal life. He became a schoolteacher in the town of Big Creek, Mississippi for six years before settling in nearby Slate Spring

Fox Connor's father, Robert, circa 1861. [Courtesy of Norm MacDonald]

Fox Connor's mother, Nannie, circa 1861. [Courtesy of Norm MacDonald]

where he accepted a job at the Slate Spring Male and Female College. The Slate Spring Male and Female College had been established in 1872 by Nannie's younger brother, Andrew Fuller Fox. Fuller was twenty-two when he founded the Slate Spring school, modeling it after his alma mater, Mansfield Male and Female College.[3] The Slate Spring school could accommodate 300 students in graded classes. It eventually became known at the Slate Spring Academy, and Bob Conner served as the superintendent.[4] Fuller taught at the school, as did his brother Basil and his sister Nannie.

Bob fell in love with Nannie and they married on December 30, 1873. They built a small wood-frame house near the campus, and Bob could easily walk to campus each day using only his cane and his other senses.[5] He knew each student by the sound of their voice and was considered one of the best teachers of those years. A wellspring of knowledge, he was admired for his grasp of scientific and historical facts and the fancies of literature.[6]

Although both of his parents were schoolteachers, they still maintained a farm for subsistence and grew hay as a cash crop. Fox Conner grew up attending Slate Spring Academy and working on the farm in his spare time. Bob and Nannie had five more children, three boys (Manly, Rush and Gus) and two girls (Mary and Nannie Gus). As the eldest son, Fox formed a special bond with his youngest sibling Nannie and they remained close until her death in 1944.

Fox grew up on stories of the Civil War, told by his father and others. Tales of epic battles and adventure made a great impression on the young boy growing up in a state steeped in the culture of military service. At the age of eight he read a report by the Secretary of War about West Point and decided he wanted to go there. At the age of twenty his dream came true.

Beginning in 1843, Congress authorized one appointment to

West Point per member of the House of Representatives.[7] Favoritism in Academy appointments was not uncommon in those days, and Fox may have benefited from this practice. By 1893 his uncle, Fuller Fox had become an influential local political, active member of the Democratic Party, and friend of Mississippi Congressman Hernando de Soto Money. After founding the Slate Spring Academy, Fuller began practicing law in 1877. In 1888, he was a delegate to the Democratic National Convention in St. Louis, where President Grover Cleveland was unanimously nominated for re-election. He served as a state Senator from 1891 to 1893, when he resigned to become the U.S. attorney for northern Mississippi.[8] Fuller Fox would replace Money in the House of Representatives when Money moved into the U.S. Senate in 1897. It's likely that Fox Conner received his nomination from Money because of his uncle's influence. On the other hand, there were no other competitors vying for Money's nomination, so Fox received a direct commission to attend West Point.[9]

Although the army was not an esteemed occupation in the late 1800s, West Point was the preferred avenue of entry for those with a military mindset. The years after the Civil War saw a shift from an officer corps composed primarily of civil appointees to West Point graduates. In 1897, graduates of West Point made up 60% of the officer corps.[10] Conner's dream of attending West Point was about to come true. He would soon learn that one should be careful what one wishes for.

June 15, 1894
West Point
The sun cast a shadow across the Hudson River and the sleepy train station just north of the town of Highland Falls, New York as Fox Conner stared up an immense hill. The gray granite rose straight up for nearly five stories from the river's edge,

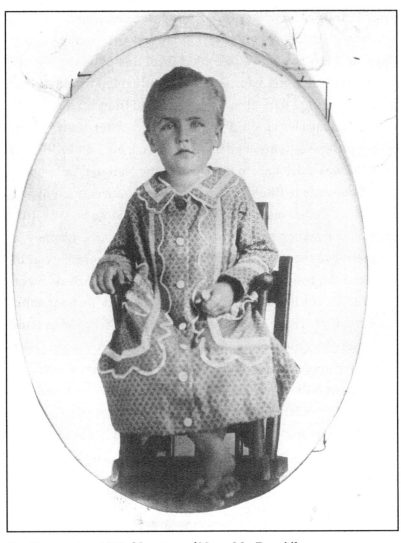

Fox Conner circa 1876. [Courtesy of Norm MacDonald]

and a small road traced a narrow route to the top. Behind him, the train slowly pulled away from the station, having fulfilled its obligation to bring new recruits to this fortress of tradition. Conner grabbed his bag and began the steep climb. He was not the first to make this journey, and he would be joined over the next twenty-four hours by 108 classmates. It had been an arduous journey from Mississippi to West Point that was, for him, over twelve months in the making. Fox's initial appointment was in 1893 but he delayed his entry by one year due to illness.[11] He used that extra year to study, knowing that the son of two schoolteachers might still find himself out of his depth at the United States Military Academy, the alma mater of nearly every general in both armies during the Civil War.

Nestled in the highlands overlooking the Hudson River, the United States Military Academy was, in 1894, eight years shy of its centennial anniversary. The history of its location and the storied glory of its graduates in the Mexican War and the Civil War had already made the Academy a legend in the public mind. The high plain at West Point commanded a strategic location overlooking the Hudson River. George Washington directed that defenses be established there to prevent the British from sailing north up the river from New York City and thereby effectively splitting the colonies. Continuously occupied by American soldiers since January 27, 1778, West Point was one of only two posts that continued to be garrisoned at the end of the Revolutionary War.[12]

Thomas Jefferson officially founded the United States Military Academy when he signed the Military Peace Establishment Act on March 16, 1802. In some ways, this official act merely served to recognize what was already a reality. A school for instruction in the military arts had existed at West Point since the Revolutionary War.[13] Presidents Washington and Adams

Conner as a cadet. [Courtesy West Point archives]

had both contemplated a formal academy at West Point. Two days before his death, George Washington replied in a letter to Alexander Hamilton's proposal for just such an institution. Hamilton had sent a plan on this subject to the Secretary of War and forwarded a copy to Washington. Washington responded that

> The Establishment of an Institution of this kind, upon a respectable and extensive basis, has ever been considered by me as an Object of primary importance to this Country; and while I was in the Chair of Government, I omitted no proper opportunity of recommending it, in my public Speeches, and otherways, [sic] to the attention of the Legislature: But I never undertook to go into a detail of the organization of such an Academy; leaving this task to others, whose pursuits in the paths of Science, and attention to the Arrangements of such Institutions, had better qualified them for the execution of it.[14]

Fox arrived and was sworn in as a cadet on June 15, 1894.[15] His home state of Mississippi had the most representation in the incoming class, contributing 5 of the 109 members of the Class of 1898.[16] Mississippi's large contingent speaks volumes about the role West Point played in reconciling the North and South following the Civil War.

The war that split the nation also split the cadets and faculty at West Point. In January 1861 President Buchanan's Secretary of War, Joseph Holt, dismissed the commander of West Point, Superintendent Pierre G.T. Beauregard, when he learned of Beauregard's plan to resign and join the Confederacy.[17] Less than three months later, Beauregard ordered the first shots of the Civil War with an artillery barrage on Fort Sumter, South Carolina. The officer defending Fort Sumter against Beauregard's forces was his former instructor of artillery, Major Robert Anderson.

For cadets from the South, loyalty to their home state often

West Point Class of 1898. [Courtesy West Point archives]

West Point Cadets marching to dinner. [Courtesy West Point archives]

superceded loyalty to the Union. Sixty-five of the 278 cadets at West Point resigned or were discharged or dismissed following the outbreak of hostilities between the North and the South in 1861.[18] Officers on the faculty left as well, and Southern graduates already serving in the Army often switched sides and fought for the Confederacy. A West Point graduate commanded forces on at least one side in the sixty major battles or campaigns fought during the Civil War, and commanded both sides in fifty-four of them.[19] West Point's alumni association, the Association of Graduates, was created in 1869 to reunite classmates who had fought against each other.[20]

Though its granite buildings give the impression of permanence, the grounds of West Point looked different in Conner's day than they do today. In 1894, roughly 250 cadets were organized into four companies, drilling and bivouacking on the parade field known as the Plain, the level plateau where Fort Clinton had stood during the Revolutionary War. Today the Corps of Cadets consists of more than four thousand cadets organized into 32 companies. The barracks building they live in today are named for generals like MacArthur, Eisenhower and Bradley who had not yet matriculated to West Point in 1894. Grant Hall, which serves as a restaurant and social gathering spot in modern times, was the mess hall for both officers and cadets in Conner's day. Cullum Hall, a neo-classical two story edifice overlooking the Hudson River which was the first home of the Association of Graduates, would not be constructed until Conner's senior year at the Academy.

In a letter he wrote home the next day after his arrival, Fox hints at the hazing that was rampant in the Corps of Cadets at the time. The upperclassmen, he writes, "make you go through all kind of monkey motions to get you straight, supple, etc. A fellow's bones ache so he can scarcely move after one of these drills." Rather than resisting the hazing, Fox seemed to relish the challenge of West Point. He writes, "I don't care how hard they are on me as it will straighten me and develop me generally," and "I like it though even better than I had expected."[21] This initial hazing took place during the summer encampment, when the cadets set up a tent city on the parade ground known as "old Ft. Clinton."[22]

Fox pleaded with his family to address any letters they wrote to "Mr. Fox Conner" instead of "Cadet Conner." To the upperclassmen, the incoming class were known as "beasts," and not considered worthy of the title "Cadet" until the start of the academic year. Because their last names were similar, Fox was targeted for additional hazing by Cadet William D. Connor, Class of 1897. Cadet Connor was concerned that poor performance on Fox's part would reflect negatively on him.[23] William Connor had nothing to fear with regard to his reputation; he would go on to graduate at the top of his class and, in 1932, become the 36th Superintendent of the Military Academy. Ironically, William and Fox could have been classmates instead of adversaries if he had reported in 1893 as initially planned.

Fox considered himself fortunate to have Alvan Chambliss Read as one of his three roommates, and in the early days of their cadet careers they aspired to stay roommates for the next four years.[24] Fox undoubtedly thought he would benefit from that arrangement in terms of his class standing, since Alvan already had a bachelor's degree and a master's degree from Louisiana State University prior to coming to West Point. In actuality, Fox graduated higher in his class than Alvan. He also graduated with a higher class standing than William Francis Nesbitt, with whom he did end up sharing a room for three of his four years at West Point.[25]

West Point has always differed greatly from traditional universities. Two systems of discipline existed simultaneously. The first was enforced by tactical officers, or "Tacs." These military officers were charged with overseeing the development of the cadets and could assign demerits to individual cadets for a host of infractions ranging from serious to picayune. Each demerit had to be "walked off" by spending one hour pacing back and forth across a courtyard between barracks buildings. Additionally, demerits were included as part of class standing. The Superintendent could dismiss a cadet who earned more than 200 demerits a year.[26]

The second system of discipline arose from the subculture within the Corps of Cadets itself. In theory, cadets were governed solely by the regulations of the Commandant and his Tacs. In practice, the upperclass cadets developed their own norms and values and enforced them physically. Cadet discipline took the form of bare fist boxing. Fourth-class cadets, or freshmen, are known as plebes. A plebe suspected of an infraction against the upperclass was required to square off against an upperclassman of similar weight. The fight continued until one of the parties couldn't stand.[27]

Daily academic life consisted of recitations in class and a heavy emphasis on math and science coupled with strict discipline and drilling to produce the nation's military officers. Plebes studied math and English in the fall. Lessons for all four classes of cadets were conducted every day except Sunday. In the spring, plebes studied math and French. As yearlings, or sophomores, cadets studied analytical and descriptive geometry, French, Spanish, and drawing. Juniors studied physics, astronomy, geology, drawing, chemistry, and began military training in the fundamentals of artillery and infantry tactics. The heavy emphasis on math during the first two years at West Point served to prepare cadets for classes in engineering as seniors. Seniors also studied law, history, cavalry tactics, and gunnery.[28]

Cadets left the Academy on furlough only once, between sophomore and junior years. Fox Conner went on furlough from noon, June 12, 1896 to 2 p.m., August 28, 1896.[29] This was his only trip home during his four years at West Point. It didn't take long for him to get used to West Point upon his return. One week later he wrote home that, "everything seems natural already. The first day or two of barracks, when we had nothing to do but get homesick, were simply awful; but they have us swing in so now that we have no time for anything except 'boning' and drilling."[30]

Fox wrote home every weekend to his parents and his little sister, Nannie Gus. His letters, invariably addressed to the "home folks," often contained little more than his grades for the week and a few details of daily cadet life. Cadets attended class in sections based on their performance and were graded daily on recitations and problems worked out with chalk on large chalkboards which dominated the classroom walls. Periodically cadets were resectioned based on the standings that were released each weekend. In a letter from his sophomore year, Fox complained that he remained in the 3rd section of math, noting that "my mark in math was the best in my section and better than over half of those in the 2nd section."[31]

In addition to academic classes, cadets also received instruction in equitation. Cadets rode for three and a half hours each Saturday and an hour each Wednesday. There is no evidence that Fox had experience with horses prior to his arrival at West Point, but he became quite proficient and enjoyed his time in the saddle. Cadets often rode to visit the home of J. Pierpont Morgan. An avid hunter himself, Fox paid particular attention to the kennels at the Morgan place during his visit.[32]

West Point Cadets walking area tours. [Courtesy West Point archives]

West Point's Cullum Hall 1899. [Courtesy West Point archives]

Fox was an average student at West Point. Though he was by all accounts studious and hard-working, at the end of each semester he would find himself ranked close to the middle of his class. He excelled more in math and science than he did in humanities classes, but his cramped and untidy writing style undoubtedly hurt him in classes like drawing and English.[33] Fox's class rank was further diminished by his disciplinary record, which was factored into class standings. He earned 384 demerits in the course of four years. Most of his delinquencies were for tardiness or smoking. He was caught on seven separate occasions smoking, each worth 5 demerits. During his plebe year, all of the plebes had 1/3 of their demerits written off by the commandant but this leniency did not extend to his next three years as a cadet.[34]

Football was a new craze at the Academy, and Fox mentioned West Point's successes and failures often in his letters home. His roommate "Weazy" Nesbitt played halfback and served as team captain of the football team, but Fox limited his role to that of a spectator. In the spring semester of his junior year, Fox began to share a room with Herbert "Goat" Lafferty. Both of their roommates from the fall semester were found deficient in academics and separated from the academy, along with three other members of the class.[35] Fox's previous roommate, Chauncey Humphrey, successfully appealed his separation and rejoined the class a week later.[36] Humphrey would go on to overcome his deficiency in Chemistry, graduate with the Class of 1898 and serve with distinction in the Army for 28 years.[37]

The Class of 1898 gained a reputation for mischief during their senior year because of their reaction to the new Commandant and one of his Tac officers. Otto Hein replaced Sam Mills as the Commandant of Cadets in 1897 and promptly forbade hazing during his tenure.[38] This prohibition was ignored by the Class of

1898 and the subculture of cadet discipline and hazing continued despite the efforts of a Tac who would prove highly influential in Fox Conner's career for years to come. First Lieutenant John J. Pershing reported to West Point on June 15, 1897, to assume duties as the Tac officer of Company A.[39]

A former First Captain of the Corps of Cadets himself, Pershing was an enthusiastic supporter of hazing, but he was also a strict enforcer of regulations. Since Hein had forbade hazing, Pershing felt honor-bound to enforce that prohibition. His zealous execution of his duties did not endear him to his company. His prior service with the Buffalo Soldiers of the 10th Cavalry earned him the nickname "Black Jack," but this is a toned down version of the original nickname which was considered much more of an insult.

In those days cadets were assigned to one of four companies based on height. Standing almost six feet tall, Fox Conner was undoubtedly a member of the infamous Company A. In later years both Pershing and Conner would write that they had known each other since Fox's cadet days and had always had the highest respect for each other. In the winter of his senior year as a cadet though, Conner would write home that Pershing was "what is known as a 'skisoid.'"[40]

Guy Henry, a member of the Class of 1898, recounted that in February 1898, members of Company A allegedly caused a bucket of water to fall on Pershing's head while he was inspecting a cadet's room.[41] According to one historian, Pershing emerged unscathed because he suspected the trick and sent a janitor into the room first. Pershing reported the incident to the Superintendent and Company A was confined to the barracks for 30 days.[42] Because of their punishment the company missed the annual Hundredth Night show, a satirical musical in which

West Point room inspection. [Courtesy West Point archives]

West Point cadets at mess. [Courtesy West Point archives]

the graduating class poked fun at themselves, their instructors, and the Academy.[43]

Fox played football on his class team, but otherwise did not participate in any extracurricular sports or clubs at West Point. This is peculiar, since most of his classmates served as members and officers of multiple clubs. The 1898 edition of the school yearbook mentions Conner only three times. Twice he is mentioned in poems that single out each graduating senior for particular traits. Fox's notable quality is his "massive brain," an interesting quote for a man who was nowhere near the top of his class academically.[44] The third entry, his senior year biography, contains slang so cryptic that it is unintelligible today even to modern West Point graduates.

> This man wears perfumery on his handkerchiefs, and tobacco on his other paraphernalia. He practices dancing with a chair on Saturday evenings, and receives a blue letter every Tuesday night. He spoons most assiduously, and bones check-book in a paying manner. From his pay of $45 per month he always saves $90. Is undoubtedly in league with Spurge.[45]

Fox's frugality had a lot to do with his family situation. Ever mindful of his family's financial circumstances, he felt obligated as the oldest son to help out. At the start of his senior year at West Point, Fox offered to help his father secure a loan to pay for the education of his five siblings. "Pa," he wrote, "if you need any money to send the chaps to school I will be glad to go on any note with you. I will have quite a little money by Oct. '98, possibly $300 or $400."[46] Saving $300 was a significant achievement for a cadet in those days. Of the $45 monthly salary cadets drew every two months, they might see approximately $15. They paid around $15 each month for board, and $8 to an equipment fund. They also contributed to the costs for damages to the mess, hospital fees, laundry, and the gas fund for heating and light.[47]

The West Point yearbook went to the publisher before the outbreak of the Spanish-American War on April 25, 1898, because it lists the graduation ceremony as June 1898. Fox's class would find themselves abruptly commissioned much sooner than that. The revolution that had been brewing in Cuba came to a head in February 1898 with the sinking of the U.S. battleship *Maine* in Havana's Harbor. On Monday April 25, 1898, Congress declared war on Spain.

That same day, the Academic Board at West Point convened at 2:30 p.m. at the request of the Superintendent to discuss a telegram from Secretary of War Alger. The Secretary had directed the Superintendent to "take the steps necessary to have the first class of the Corps of Cadets graduated as soon as merit rolls and diplomas can be prepared."[48] After a brief discussion, the Academic Board voted to have the first class graduate the next day. The department heads undoubtedly had a long night of work, since the order of merit roll for the class of 1898 had to be calculated overnight by hand.

As the Academic Board met to discuss the telegram, Fox and his classmates were attending a law lecture given by Colonel George Davis, the head of the Department of Law and History. An orderly disturbed the lecture to deliver a message to Colonel Davis. After reading it, he addressed Fox and his peers. "Gentlemen," he said, "I will not continue. You may return to your quarters; you will graduate tomorrow, noon."[49] As it turned out, the class would have to wait an additional five hours for their freedom. The Superintendent decreed that graduation exercises would commence in the chapel at 5 p.m. on April 26, 1898.[50]

Fox Conner graduated from West Point on April 26, 1898 along with 58 classmates. Within four years, five of his classmates would be killed in action, die of wounds, or perish on ships headed to the front.[51] Fox left West Point with $323.25. Of that sum, $184 was the equipment fund set aside to purchase his Army gear. This equipment fund had been set aside in $8 increments each pay period.[52]

Conner graduated high in his class but didn't get a cavalry commission as he wished. Some have asserted, incorrectly, that he was not high enough in his class to get a cavalry commission. In fact, Fox had ranked 3rd in the class in cavalry tactics as recently as March, 1898.[53] He graduated 17th in a class of 59 and was recommended based on his rank for a commission in artillery, cavalry, or infantry.[54] The actual reason Conner didn't become a cavalryman had more to do with the needs of the Army. Conner's classmate, Guy Henry, noted that there were no vacancies for second lieutenants in cavalry at the time of their commission.[55] Henry would eventually transfer to cavalry, compete in the 1912 Olympics as a rider, and become the Chief of Cavalry in the 1930s. Conner was commissioned as a Second Lieutenant of Artillery and assigned to Fort Adams, Rhode Island. He continued trying to transfer to cavalry until 1899, writing four separate requests. Despite recommendations of his superiors, each request was denied.[56] Conner was destined to be an artilleryman, and he became one of the greatest artillery experts of the twentieth century.

Chapter Two
Warrior Journeyman

Cuba

Despite the urgency with which the Class of 1898 graduated, it would be almost a year before Fox Conner joined the American forces in Cuba. After one month of leave, he reported to Battery D of the 2nd U.S. Artillery on May 25, 1898. His regimental commander, Lieutenant Colonel William Haskin, carried Conner on the rolls as "temporarily attached" because he was only authorized one 2nd lieutenant per battery during peacetime and wartime authorizations had not yet taken effect.[57] Haskin made a considerable impression on Conner as his first commanding officer. A graduate of Rensselear Polytechnic Institute in Troy, New York, Haskin was a veteran of the Civil War, a voracious reader and prolific writer. While commanding an artillery battery in 1897 at the Presidio of Monterey, California, Haskin wrote *The History of the First Regiment of Artillery*, a massive 668 page tome.[58] It is likely that Haskin's interest in military history, philosophy, poetry and prose inspired Conner in the same way that he would inspire Dwight Eisenhower two decades later.

Fort Adams jutted out from the city of Newport, Rhode Island, on a small peninsula overlooking Narragansett Bay. Conner did not stay at Fort Adams for long, however, and soon after arriving he was put in charge of a coastal artillery detachment at Clark's Point, Massachusetts. Throughout the summer of 1898 Conner guarded the New England coast, drilling his men to ensure they were ready for the Spanish fleets that never materialized. Meanwhile, Major General William Shafter led the successful invasion of Cuba and the war in Cuba was finished before the end of July. Conner had missed the war but he would soon experience the occupation.

In September 1898 Conner joined Battery A of the 2nd Artillery at Camp Wheeler, Alabama, where he served under Captain George Grimes.[59] Grimes and the men of Battery A had seen action on San Juan Hill and had endured ten straight days of combat before returning to the U.S. for rest and refit.[60] Conner also served as battalion adjutant for the 2nd Artillery, and on January 21, 1899, he boarded a ship bound for Camp Columbia, Havana, Cuba.[61] The large number of volunteers in the Cuban occupation meant that Conner spent most of his time on basic troop training and discipline. Each day brought new challenges, but Conner was excited to be working for men like Haskin and Grimes. In his spare time he studied to prepare for his promotion examinations and improved his Spanish.[62]

On Monday, June 25, 1900, General Haskin presided over the board of five officers examining Conner for promotion. Conner was pleased to see that Captain Grimes was also a member of his promotion board.[63] He scored an average of 86.8. His highest scores were drill regulations and administration, not surprising for someone who had spent most of the previous year as an adjutant. His lowest were military topography and minor tactics, which is also not very surprising considering the difficulty he had with drawing as a cadet. Conner was certified for promotion to 1st Lieutenant, but the board noted that he had "considerable room for increased technical knowledge of artillery and military engineering." [64]

"Bug"

Evenings in Cuba were taken up with parties, dinners, and social gatherings where the Cuban upper class mixed with American officers and businessmen. Young American women flocked to Cuba to experience the exotic nature of the Caribbean and perhaps attract the attention of a dashing young officer. If they had set their eyes on Fox Conner, however, they were bound to be disappointed. Although Conner attended these gatherings, he preferred the company of other soldiers. He did not like to dance and earned a reputation as a woman-hater. These qualities only increased the determination of one young woman named Bug.[65]

Her name was Virginia Grahame Brandreth, but everyone in the family called her "Bug." Born into a wealthy New York family in December, 1879, Bug was the second of four children sired by Colonel Franklin Brandreth. His father, Dr. Benjamin Brandreth, made his fortune in the patent medicine business with an over-the-counter cure for indigestion known as Brandreth Pills. The family's real estate holdings included 25,000 acres in the Adirondacks of upstate New York and the family compound in Ossining where Bug grew up.[66] Colonel Brandreth was an avid outdoorsman. He was the first lifetime member of the Sing Sing Yacht Club and also belonged to the New York Yacht Club.[67] Bug enjoyed the type of upbringing common for women of her station, being trained in classical music and homemaking skills, but she also inherited a sense of adventure and independence from her father. Her aunt Florence, who had married a military man, invited Bug to visit them in Cuba. Initially Franklin refused to allow the visit, but Bug had a cold at the time and her mother convinced him that the warm climate would be good for her. Eventually he relented and it was during that fateful trip in early 1900 that Bug met Fox Conner.[68]

Bug spent two months in Cuba, riding horses by day and attending parties at night. It was at one of these parties, hosted by her uncle Herbert Slocum, that she noticed Fox Conner. She talked to some of the other women and learned of his "woman-hater" reputation. That was enough of a challenge for twenty-one year old Bug and she set her sights on gaining his affection.[69] She returned to New York in time for the spring social season.

The next time they met was one year later in March 1901 when Bug came to Washington, DC, for President McKinley's inauguration. Conner was stationed at Washington Barracks (now known as Fort McNair), a common posting for bachelor officers in a capitol that flourished on society parties and fancy dinners.[70] The officers in their formal uniforms added a sense of dash to evening functions, so attendance was often compulsory. By now Fox had passed his promotion examination for first lieutenant.[71] Having been spurned in Cuba, Bug had set her sights on Conner and this time, the feelings of affection were mutual. She spent three weeks visiting him though they were heavily chaperoned and barely had a moment alone until the last day. When they were finally alone he invited her to come watch his upcoming exhibition in New York City.

During the week beginning on Monday, March 25, 1901, Conner's battery was scheduled to perform at Madison Square Garden. This was the Fourth Battery, Field Artillery, from Washington Barracks under Captain Parkhurst and Lieutenant Conner. Also performing were cadet riders from West Point under the direction of Captain Sands, infantry from Governor's Island under Lieutenant Phillips, and engineers from Willet's Point under Conner's old nemesis from his plebe days, Lieutenant William D. Connor.[72]

Though there was undoubtedly an attraction, this invitation

was probably also something of a test. By this time Conner knew how difficult the military lifestyle could be on a spouse, and he wanted to see if Bug had the independence an Army wife would need to endure the hardship assignments he was destined to receive. He gave Bug tickets to the performance but told her he could not escort her from Ossining to New York City. If this was a test, she passed with flying colors, not only attending but bringing her mother and her sister to meet Fox. He was now as smitten as she was and proposed to Bug that spring during a cruise on the Potomac River.

He visited Ossining for the first time on July 4, 1901, and asked her father for her hand.[73] Two months earlier he had passed the promotion examination for captain.[74] He had originally been ordered to serve as the recorder for the promotion board which met in May 1901 at Fort Myer, Virginia.[75] At the last minute, however, he was relieved of his duties by Lieutenant Edward Timberlake and ordered instead to present himself to the board for consideration.[76] The board dispensed with written examinations and Conner passed with flying colors.[77] His next challenge was convincing Colonel Brandreth to give his consent to the match.

Brandreth had often said that marrying an Army man was the one thing he would not allow his daughters to do. Bug's autobiography, published in 1950, was appropriately entitled, *What Father Forbad*. Despite his rule about military sons-in-law, however, Franklin and Fox liked each other at their first meeting and became lifelong friends.[78] Cliff Cottage, the Brandreth family home, became a second home for Fox and the retreat to which he would later bring luminaries like Pershing and Marshall to hunt and fish.

The wedding took place eleven months later on June 4, 1902.

"Fox and Bug" sketch; Bug is the artist. [Courtesy of Norm MacDonald]

By this time Conner was the commander of the 123rd Company of Coastal Artillery at Fort Hamilton, New York, a much closer duty station than Washington, DC.[79] Fox Conner and Virginia were married at Cliff Cottage in an evening ceremony that was covered in the society pages of the *New York Times*. All of the officers present were in full uniform for the military ceremony and the house was decorated with military memorabilia. Fox being an artilleryman, it's no surprise that the color red, the official color of the branch, dominated the decorations.

Reverend George Wilson Ferguson, the rector of Trinity Church, performed the ceremony. Mr. Ferguson, as he liked to be called, had known Bug since her birth.[80] He had led the church for 34 years and had officiated at her grandfather's funeral in 1880.[81] At the time of the wedding, the church's parish hall was still being constructed which may have been the reason the wedding was held at Cliff Cottage. The reception took place in the adjoining smoking room. The bride, dressed in a gown of peau de soie trimmed with duchess lace, was attended by her sister Paulina as well as a friend and two cousins. Conner's friend George Barney served as his best man and six other officers acted as ushers and escorts: Captain Marcellus G. Spinks, Captain Lee Roy Lyon, Captain Henry W. Butner, Lieutenant C.C. Carter, Lieutenant Harry Wilbur, and Lieutenant William P. Ennis.[82] Bug's father promised to continue her allowance of $200 a month, which more than doubled their income since Conner's monthly salary as a captain was only $165.[83]

Fort Leavenworth

In the summer of 1905, Fox received orders to the Staff School at Fort Leavenworth, Kansas. He took a train west and reported for duty in July. Bug stayed behind in New York to give birth to their second child, Fox Brandreth Conner, born on June 23, 1905.[84] Their daughter Betty Virginia (Betsey) was nineteen months old. Bug spent the rest of the summer at the Brandreth camp in the Adirondacks, as was her custom, and brought the children to join Fox in the fall.

Perching on the western edge of the Missouri River, Fort Leavenworth had been the home of the Infantry and Cavalry School since 1881. The initial purpose for the school was to train lieutenants for duties in units larger than companies. By 1893, the school's curriculum had expanded to a two-year program taught by seven academic departments within what was called the General Service and Staff College. The Department of Military Art taught classes in international law and military history, and the faculty used map problems to teach strategy and grand tactics at the corps, division and brigade level.[85] Although the school languished during the Spanish-American War, it was under new management by the time Fox Conner arrived. Franklin Bell, a veteran of the Philippines who had risen from lieutenant to brigadier general in five years, became the commandant of the college in 1903 and instituted a return to the curriculum of the 1890s.[86]

Until the 1905-1906 class, no artillery officers had entered the Infantry and Cavalry School or the Staff College.[87] Special orders from the War Department detailed Fox Conner and two other artillerymen, Samuel C. Vestal and Henry W. Butner, to the Staff College. These three men had the honor of being the first to enter the Staff College and also the last to be admitted without completing the competitive course of the Infantry and Cavalry School.[88] Their admittance to the College was a controversial experiment by the Army. General Bell, a Medal of Honor recipient who had been promoted directly from captain to brigadier general, was convinced that any artilleryman who entered the Staff College without "the advantage of the course in the Infantry and Cavalry School [was] seriously handicapped in his college work, and [was] rarely if ever able to overcome this handicap." He did not believe that the artillery officers would be able to achieve a high degree of efficiency in the work of the Staff College.[89] Nevertheless, both General Bell and the War College selection committee were willing to make the attempt.

The Leavenworth schools were intended to be the essential rungs of the ladder for every officer seeking entry into the War College, and up to that time the Artillery had been excluded from that place on the career track. If Conner was aware of the perceived challenge in this assignment, he could have found strength in the memories of his plebe year at West Point. During his days as a cadet he felt his schooling at Slate Springs Academy was inadequate compared to the preparatory education of many of his classmates. Conner's ambition and hard work, however, saw him through the Military Academy. Now, with five and a half years of administrative and command experience, he felt capable of completing the Staff College course.

Students at the Staff College noticed one particular problem with the curriculum. There were no maps of North America, so map problems were worked out on German maps of the Metz region. Many students protested using these maps of the Franco-German border. Some of the disgruntled students included John Palmer and Fox Conner. Their study of these maps would come in handy, however, when they found themselves planning operations on the very same ground during World War I.

Conner excelled at the Staff College despite his lack of training at the Infantry and Cavalry School. He particularly enjoyed working for General Bell, and would serve under his tutelage as a student, instructor, and staff officer for most of the next six years. For his part, Bell saw tremendous potential in Conner. Some of that may have been a reflection of the similarities in their backgrounds. Bell was born in rural Kentucky to a family of Confederate veterans. He struggled as a cadet at West Point, graduating in 1878 ranked 38th in a class of 43. A cavalryman, Bell shared Conner's love for horses. Bell also served as a role model for Conner as a self-taught professional officer who read French, Spanish, and German.

Bug did not enjoy Fort Leavenworth. The Staff College was an extremely demanding program and Fox studied seven days a week. When he wasn't in class or working with his study group, he was ensconced in his study in their small two-story quarters with his books and maps. She spent most of her time raising their two children. She found little comfort in the company of the other wives, noting in her memoirs that:

> There was nothing for the wives to do as all had cooks and some, myself included, had nurses. We wasted precious hours playing cards. I have always hated the abuse of anything that is done for pleasure – smoking, drinking or endlessly playing contract bridge as many of my contemporaries do today in Washington. What is fun done in moderation is bad when done to excess.[90]

The Life of Riley

His hard work paid off when Fox graduated in the summer of 1906. General Bell gave him a glowing efficiency report and recommended him for a teaching assignment at Fort Leavenworth, West Point, or the War College.[91] Then, as now, however, the Army did not always follow the recommendations of senior officers. The artillery branch had a shortage of officers at Fort

Captain Fox Conner on the firing range. [Courtesy of Norm MacDonald]

Riley, Kansas, and Conner soon found himself assigned as the post adjutant under his former commander from Cuba, Colonel George Grimes.[92]

For Bug, Fort Riley was a welcome respite from Leavenworth. Her uncle, Major Herbert Slocum, and her beloved aunt Bird were also stationed at Riley with the 2nd Cavalry. If it hadn't been for Bird's invitation to visit Cuba, Bug might not have ever met Conner. At last she had a companion with whom to go riding when Fox was on maneuvers, and they enjoyed the next seven months together. When the weather was nice the post offered trails across fertile valleys, flatlands and grassy hills. When the harsh Midwest winter came, they would utilize the post's indoor riding hall.[93] Aunt Bird's company helped to compensate for the long hours Fox was working.

The artillery branch was undergoing drastic changes in the aftermath of the Spanish-American war. In August 1905, the Army had designated Fort Riley as the primary center of training for the Field Artillery branch.[94] Colonel Grimes and his staff were tasked to develop new tactics and doctrine for the branch and new training curriculum despite the funding cutbacks that were a traditional outcome of American isolationism following war. This type of challenge was one that Conner was particularly suited for, having spent a year at Leavenworth examining problems of tactics, doctrine, and training.

The spring and summer of 1907 found Conner serving as post adjutant, instructor, and umpire for the annual training maneuvers at Fort Riley. Brigadier General Theodore Wint, a veteran of the Civil War and the Indian Wars, oversaw the exercise involving artillery units from Nebraska to Arkansas as they rotated through Fort Riley. Wint noted in a 1907 memorandum that Fox Conner "rendered invaluable service in the work of preparing suitable problems for the artillery. He is a diligent, valuable officer."[95]

Conner was also learning the skills necessary to be a chief of operations, a position that did not exist in the Army at the time but one which he would become the exemplar of under Pershing. Today, the position of adjutant in an Army unit deals largely with ceremonies, protocol, personnel and finance issues. In Conner's day, the adjutant was a catch-all position, requiring an officer who could speak authoritatively in the absence of the commander on topics ranging from logistics and supply to training and doctrine. It also required an officer who could work well with the unit chief of staff. Fox's time at Leavenworth had prepared him well for this assignment, and he would bring all of these skills to bear again in 1917.

Conner's superior performance attracted attention at the highest levels of the Army, and he was assigned as an instructor at the War College in DC in September 1907. En route from Fort Riley he took a well deserved forty-day leave with his family at the Brandreth estate in the Adirondacks.[96] On September 3, 1907, he moved to Washington Barracks for his assignment on the General Staff Third Division and as an instructor at the Army War College.[97]

Army War College

Teddy Roosevelt's Secretary of War, Elihu Root, envisioned the Army War College as both a post-graduate course in the science of war and an operational adjunct to the War Department General Staff.[98] Created in 1903, the Army War College was located in the nation's capitol. Brigadier General Tasker Bliss, a West Point graduate who had served on the faculty of the Naval War College, was the first President of the War College. Bliss incorporated elements of the Naval War College and the Prussian *Kriegsakademie* into the new institution. Officers selected to attend the College had already learned the duties associated with troop units as students at Leavenworth's Staff College. Now they would learn the duties of a staff officer at the highest level of the Army, the General Staff.[99] As a record-keeping measure, officers were assigned to the War College as students and to the General Staff Corps as faculty.

Conner graduated from the War College in 1908 and was assigned to the Army General Staff with teaching duties at the Army War College. In his first year at the War College, the institution was still evolving. Only five years old as an institution, the War College had not yet achieved Root's vision and suffered from a lack of faculty members. By his third year teaching, Conner undoubtedly had more experience than some of his students but they had more rank. As a captain, Conner found himself lecturing to majors, lieutenant colonels, and colonels. One of his students, Colonel Hunter Liggett, had graduated from West Point nine years earlier than Conner.

Conner's superior performance as a student and instructor attracted the attention of three high-ranking officers in Washington, Wotherspoon, Bliss, and Bell. Brigadier General William W. Wotherspoon had served as Director of the War College under Bliss and his successor, Brigadier General Thomas Barry. A veteran of the Philippines, Wotherspoon became President of the War College in October 1907. By this time Tasker Bliss had risen to become Assistant Chief of Staff of the Army. General Bell knew Conner from his days as a student at Fort Leavenworth. After spending the summer of 1908 on an exchange program at the Naval War College, Conner found himself working for Bliss at Bell's request.

In addition to lecturing at the War College, Conner now found himself organizing staff rides to Civil War battlefields, overseeing individual student research projects, developing artillery doctrine from his experiences in Fort Riley's training maneuvers, and serving on research committees studying the conduct of officer training at other Army posts. In the summer of 1909 he sent Bug and the children to the Brandreth family camp and reported to Governor's Island in New York Harbor to participate in the largest maneuver exercise in Army history.

General Bliss commanded the attacking Red Army against Brigadier General William Pew's Blue Army, whose task it was to defend the major urban centers of the East coast. Over 20,000 Regular Army and militia troops took part in the seven-day war game which began on August 13. The war game tested the feasibility of using radio, known as wireless telephone, and automobiles in war.[100] As a result of his performance in the maneuvers, Conner received a formal commendation from General Bliss.[101]

Conner also began writing articles for publication in professional military journals while serving on the General Staff. In May 1910 he published an article in the *Journal of the United States Infantry Association* entitled, "Field Artillery in Cooperation with the Other Arms." This article became the basis for revisions to the Field Artillery Drill Regulations manual the next year and confirmed Conner's reputation as the Army's expert on artillery. In 1911, Conner also joined Captains John Palmer and Matthew Hanna in proposing a single list promotion bill. At that time, promotion was based on one's position on an order-of-merit list within one's branch. Palmer advocated combining the seniority lists of the artillery, infantry, cavalry, and engineers into one list. He believed that as an infantry officer, his advocacy of the legislation would be suspicious to officers in the other branches because the proposal appeared to benefit the infantry branch in which peacetime promotion was very slow. To anticipate this criticism, Palmer enlisted Conner's help as an artilleryman and Hanna's help as a cavalryman. They each prepared statements in which they expressed their approval of the single list bill. All three items were published in the *Army and Navy Journal* in July 1911.[102] The article drew a vast response, both positive and negative. The majority of negative responses came from the artillery, according to Palmer.[103] While this provocative group of articles was being perused by his colleagues, Fox would be sailing the Atlantic Ocean on his way to France.

France

The last two years in Washington had been professionally fulfilling for Conner but had taken a toll on his family. Even with Bug's monthly allowance, Conner's salary was barely sufficient in the expensive capitol city. Bug's beloved Aunt Bird was killed in a car accident while visiting DC in 1910. Conner often worked to the point of physical exhaustion despite Bug's concern for his health. Maneuvers and inspections of other posts kept him away for weeks at a time. To add to the stress, their third child was born on October 31, 1910. Bug named their daughter Florence in honor of her Aunt Bird.

As his time in Washington drew to a close, Fox began to look for a new assignment. He was offered several positions. General Barry, the former President of the War College, was Superintendent at West Point at the time. He wanted Conner to be the senior instructor of Artillery tactics. Conner was also offered a posting as an attaché in both Turkey and Mexico.[104] Then General Wotherspoon offered Conner a job he could not resist. Would he be interested in serving as an exchange officer to a French Artillery Regiment and attending the French War College, *Le Ecole Superieure de Guerre*? Bug was visiting family in Ossining at the time but Conner knew she would not object. The chance to live in France was the opportunity of a lifetime. Conner said yes.[105] Both Fox and Bug could read French, but they were less confident in their ability to speak the language. Fox enrolled in a course at the famed Berlitz school and Bug hired a private tutor in Ossining. They sailed for Antwerp in July of 1911 on a Red Star oceanliner, along with Betsey, Tommy, Florence, and a wetnurse.[106]

When the Conners sailed for Europe, the continent was divided into two contentious alliances bristling with armaments. The Triple Alliance - Germany, Austria-Hungary and Italy - and the Entente Cordiale of Britain, Russia and France were elbowing their way to war. The German general staff under Field Marshal von Schleiffen had been studying ways to invade and defeat France since 1905. The generals continued to hone their strategy, believing that war was not only inevitable but desirable. France anticipated this German assault. Fired by a desire for revenge over the humiliation of the Franco-Prussian War in 1870, the French General Staff designed plans for a massive counter-thrust into the heart of Germany. Thirty years prior, European armies had numbered in the thousands; now they numbered in the millions.

The Conners loved their time in France. They experienced the trials and tribulations that many others have had while traveling but both had a positive attitude and treated the experience as an adventure. The military and naval attachés in Paris were both personal friends of the Conners, but they were on vacation when Fox and Bug arrived from Antwerp. Needing a place to stay, they booked rooms at the Hotel Vatel in Versailles. Fox established an account at the Credit Lyonaise bank, but the bank would not allow him to draw money immediately because his paychecks had not yet cleared. Fox didn't want to seek help from the embassy, because he was the first American to participate in this exchange program. Instead, Bug's father came to their assistance and arranged to send them money through the family business's office in Birkenhead, England.[107] Eventually, they leased a house, Villa les Violettes, 6 rue Deschamps, Versailles.[108] Fox's service with the 22nd Artillery Regiment didn't officially begin until October, so the family spent two months traveling and getting acquainted with Paris.

Once he reported to his unit, Conner threw himself into his work while Bug managed the household with her French servant, Marie, who served as maid, nanny, and cook. The Conners also employed a housekeeper. Betsy and Tommy went first to a French public school, but Tommy was frightened because he could not speak French. Because of Tommy's distress, Fox and Bug took the children to a small expatriate school attended mostly by English children.[109]

Conner spent long hours into the evenings in his study, but occasionally he took the afternoon off and the family visited art galleries and museums.[110] When he went on maneuvers with the French, Bug would bundle the children off to Switzerland.[111] Back in Versailles, Bug felt fortunate to have Marie as a nanny and spent many pleasant days wandering the streets of Paris. She was especially fond of the left bank of the Seine and its bohemian atmosphere. The evenings were when Bug felt her "real work started, for it was no joke to try to teach the children Bible, history, and arithmetic in French." After putting the children to bed, Fox and Bug would settle in the sitting room with a bottle of wine and talk before he went up to his study.

With the 22nd Artillery, Conner was involved daily in planning and field operations. On maneuvers he got to use the best piece of field artillery in the world, the 75 millimeter field gun or "soixante quinze," to learn the modern principles of artillery in combat. Conner was amazed by the design of the French cannon, dubbed the "Father, Son, and Holy Ghost" by French gunners. Using the principle of the gun's recoiling on its carriage, the French artillery workshops secured an increase in muzzle energy more than double that of the U.S. Army's three-inch gun which was designed on the same recoil principle. The French achieved that greater performance with less increase in weight than the American gun as well. The American artillery piece had a slower rate of fire, lower muzzle velocity and required the gunner to re-aim after firing each round. In contrast, the French gunners could fire their cannon from 15 to 30 times per minute without having to re-aim the gun. [112] In six years, Conner would be called upon by the Army as their artillery expert, and what he knew about the relative merits of French and American artillery would have a major impact on American policy.

While in France, Conner also witnessed the controversial discussions within the French government about weapons procurement. On one side of the debate was the French Army, which favored the 75-millimeter field gun in both attack and defense over heavier artillery pieces like the 105-millimeter field gun.[113] On the other side was the French War Council, which proposed to add great numbers of the 105-millimeter heavy field cannon to the army's inventory. Artillerymen scorned the heavy guns because they believed that those weapons, like the machine gun, were defensive weapons, and that too much emphasis on defense was detrimental to the offensive spirit. The French Field Artillery was also concerned that the heavier gun would impede the physical movement of the assaulting forces. In their mind, the power of the French Army lay in the speed of its offensive capability; the élan with which the combined forces of infantry and light field artillery struck the enemy.[114]

French field regulations prescribed tactics of assault that relied on the artillery striking with a storm of shrapnel to force the enemy infantry to take cover. After sufficient but minimal preparation fire to establish proper firing data, French batteries from masked positions were directed to open fire over the heads of their advancing infantry, hitting the enemy before he could return fire. The intermittent fire would sweep the area forcing the defenders below ground.[115] The French calculated that the attacking infantry could race 50 meters in about 20 seconds before the enemy soldiers could recover, shoulder and fire their rifles.[116]

Tactical exercises in the field afforded to Conner invaluable experience with the terrain where his new comrades of the 22nd Field Artillery Regiment would fight. In classrooms, he studied the strategy and plans of attack of the French Army, and he soon realized that French strategists were also divided into two camps.[117] Each acknowledged a great German assault would come through Belgium into northern France, but they disagreed on how France should respond. One group favored a defensive strategy which anchored the right wing of the French defense with the fortified region of Lorraine in eastern France and extended a defensive line of one million Frenchmen from Verdun northwest to Antwerp. The second group wanted to concentrate the French Army's offensive power in the east facing Alsace-Lorraine, which at the time belonged to Germany. After the German assault through Belgium, the French would hold the line on the Franco-Belgian border while the bulk of the French

Virginia "Bug" Brandreth and her sister, Beatrice, circa 1880s. [Courtesy of Norm MacDonald]

Circa 1909–from left to right: Fox Conner, Virginia "Bug" Brandreth, Beatrice and Fred Hahn, at Camp Brandreth. [Courtesy of Norm MacDonald]

Conner's library at Camp Good Enough, Brandreth, NY. Ann Wilson (family friend) is pictured seated. [Courtesy of Norm MacDonald]

forces would drive north through Alsace and Lorraine advancing into the industrial heart of the Saar region along the quickest, shortest route into Germany, cutting the German Army's lines of communication. This latter strategy was adopted by the French government in 1913 and named Plan XVII.[118]

Conner was scheduled to attend the French War College in the fall of 1912 but did not attend. In August, Congress passed what was known as the "Manchu Law," requiring company-grade officers to spend two years out of every six with troops.[119] "Manchu" was a slang term applied by Army officers in the field to the chair-bound officers who were on permanent duty in the bureaus of the War Department. In their opinion, the Army bureaucrats sat like officials of the Manchu Dynasty, secluded and isolated from the people they ruled.[120] Conner had not served with troops since his time at Fort Riley in 1907. Much to his dismay and Bug's, he was ordered home from France without the opportunity to attend the French War College. Conner would not be there to see Plan XVII put into action during the outbreak of World War I. Instead he would find himself in the border town of Laredo, Texas, chasing an elusive Mexican general named José Doroteo Arango Arámbula, better known as Pancho Villa.

The Life of Riley and Bliss

In October 1912 Conner was once more assigned to Fort Riley, Kansas, this time as part of the Sixth Field Artillery Regiment. Five years after his first tour at Fort Riley, Conner was even more impressive as an officer because of his time on the General Staff and in France. He passed his promotion board examination for the rank of Major in April 1913 but faced a three-year wait on the seniority list. In the meantime he commanded E battery.[121] The following July he also commanded the Camp of Instruction for

Militia Field Artillery officers.[122] This training camp was similar to the maneuver exercises he had organized as the post adjutant in 1907. He was commended by the commanding general of the post, who recommended that Conner be named the alternative officer to take charge of the following year's camp. His recommendation was followed, and Conner was scheduled to have command of the camp scheduled for the first two weeks of June, 1914.[123] Instead, he found himself in the desert sands along the Texas border.

Trouble had been brewing on the border with Mexico since the spring of 1911. In 1910 Francisco Madero had defeated Mexican president Porfirio Diaz in a major victory for his revolutionary forces. Madero promised to reform the government but did not act quickly enough for more radical revolutionaries in his government. He was forced to resign the presidency in 1913 by Victoriano Huerta, the commander of the Mexican army. Years of turmoil followed as rebels like Francisco "Pancho" Villa and Álvaro Obregón fought Huerta and each other. In response, the United States positioned a force of almost 7,000 men on the Mexican border to patrol from Texas to Arizona to prevent the conflict from spilling over into American territory. This force patrolled the border with a complement of six regiments of Cavalry, 1½ regiments of Infantry, a battalion of field artillery accompanied by a couple of companies from the Coast Artillery and a company of the Signal Corps. Conner's unit would become part of that vast desert army in the spring of 1914.

In April 1914, General John J. Pershing assumed command of the American forces in the El Paso Military District. Rumors that Francisco Villa was making a forced march on El Paso caused the United States to deploy Conner's regiment to the Texas-Mexico border. Under the command of Lt. Col. William L. Kenly, the

Regimental Headquarters and First Battalion were placed on alert. After several frantic, false alarms they were loaded onto trains by mid-afternoon on April 24. On the station platform surrounded by families of the departing battalion waving and shouting their farewells, the regimental band played the *Campbells are Coming*, until the last car left the post. After two days of traveling they reached Fort Bliss, a desolate border post near the town of El Paso, Texas.[124] They participated in an extravagant parade orchestrated by Pershing as a show of strength to both the citizens of El Paso and any watching enemies. That parade also included nine troops of the 13th Cavalry, seven troops of the 15th Cavalry, four troops of the 12th Cavalry, and the 6th, 16th and 20th Infantry Regiments plus Battery B of the 3rd Field Artillery.[125]

For Conner, who was in the Second Battalion, the night of April 23rd was chaotic. Bug and her friends were presenting a musical at the Officer's Club when he entered the room with the news that the entire regiment was being sent to Texas. He had heard it from Associated Press reports on the radio, and as they walked to their quarters the news was confirmed by the regimental adjutant. The adjutant told Fox that railroad cars would arrive first thing in the morning.[126] The post heard the news from the AP because, when Colonel Kenly received the telegraphed orders, he decided to wait until next morning to inform the regiment, so that the troops should have a good night's rest.

Conner spent the night packing. His days were full of administrative and training duties, and he had not anticipated having to access his field gear until the summer maneuvers in June. His equipment was in the attic, scattered among various boxes. To make matters worse, a sudden thunderstorm pounded the post, thundering against the attic roof just inches overhead. Bug quietly watched Fox tear through the mounds of household goods looking for all of his pieces of kit. The thunderstorm woke Betsey, who was afraid that her newborn guinea pigs would drown in the downpour. "Fox went out and returned soaked, but with the entire litter safe in one hand."[127]

At dawn on the 24th, the entire post waited for the 1st Battalion to embark, and when it finally pulled out of the station, the 2nd Battalion loaded onto the train late in the afternoon and evening. As they waited, Bug wrote of her frustration and anxiety, "Fox would kiss me good-bye and in an hour be back to say that the trains had not yet arrived. This went on all day and when they finally came, they had to be loaded in the dark."[128]

Conner and his battery arrived at the sleepy town of Laredo, Texas, on April 28th. While the battalion headquarters stayed at Laredo, Conner's battery occupied nearby Fort McIntosh. Established in 1849 to defend the American border at the Rio Bravo river, Fort McIntosh had been abandoned and reoccupied throughout the Civil War. Though it would undergo construction to accommodate an influx of 15,000 soldiers during World War I as a training camp, in 1914 Fort McIntosh was predominantly a tent city. Lucian Truscott wrote of the camp that it was a "sea of canvas," next to a parade field used for drill "where desert winds raised spiraling clouds of dust when drilling troops did not."[129] For the next six months, Conner's battery conducted long and exhausting patrols along the border attached to infantry or cavalry units.

In October, 1914 a shortage of commanding officers for newly mobilized units caused him to be transferred to the Fifth Artillery Regiment at Fort Sill, Oklahoma. Bug and the children, who had left Fort Riley to spend the summer in New York, joined him at

Fort Sill but their reunion was short-lived.[130] Within months he was back on the border commanding a battery of the Fifth Artillery, this time in Naco, Arizona. On January 1, 1915, Prohibition began in Arizona. Commanders like Conner had to contend with soldiers and civilians who sought to cross the border to Naco, Sonora, Mexico in search of alcohol.[131] Relief from border duty came the following summer, when the commandant of the School of Fire at Fort Sill requested Captain Conner as an instructor.

In 1902 the field artillery branch had moved from Fort Riley, Kansas to Fort Sill, Oklahoma. Located in the heart of what was once Indian country, Fort Sill was one of the most isolated posts in the Army at the time. The vast emptiness of land around it made it seem like the ideal location to perfect the practice of artillery fire. Lieutenant Colonel Ed McGlachlin, the commander of the Fifth Artillery Regiment, also served as the commandant of the Artillery School known as the School of Fire. Conner's performance as one of his battery commanders attracted his notice.[132]

By July 1915, Conner began teaching as a senior instructor training new officers in the intricacies of employing artillery cannons. This assignment gave him the opportunity to work with another talented officer who would rise to fame in the coming years, Captain Leslie McNair. He and Conner knew each other from assignments as students, but this was their first opportunity to work together. McNair led the statistical department of the school and sought to compile data from all of the live-fire exercises for analysis.

In addition to teaching, Conner continued to be involved in seeking out new technology for the Army. After a few weeks at Sill, he was ordered by the Field Artillery Board to the Southwest Tractor Show in Enid, Oklahoma.[133] Conner was charged with evaluating caterpillar tractors for possible use towing artillery pieces. A few years later during World War I, a caterpillar tractor used to pull artillery pieces would inspire a British colonel named Ernest Swinton to design the first armored tank.

That same summer Conner helped with airplane testing at Fort Sill as well. The Army's first air unit, the 1st Aero Squadron, arrived at Fort Sill in August 1915. The airmen who flew the Curtiss JN-2, known as the Jenny, worked with Conner and other artillerymen to perfect techniques for directing artillery fires from the air. With his knowledge of topography, Conner was a logical choice to evaluate the aerial photos and maps the Jennies began to produce of Fort Sill. Life continued quietly at Fort Sill while a border war simmered and Europe fell into chaos. Soon events would pull Conner away from the quiet life and onto the world stage through an unusual route, the Inspector General's office.

An Inspector General

Within the Army staff, the task of ensuring adherence with regulations fell to the Inspector General's office, or IGO. Since 1901, the IGO had followed a practice of borrowing officers from line units for a specified tour of duty and then returning them to their branch. The IGO benefitted from each officer's expertise and the Army benefitted by the ability to keep the permanent staff of the IGO small. That balance was upset in March 1916.

The tenuous situation on the Mexican border took a turn for the worse on March 9, 1916, when Pancho Villa launched an attack on Columbus, New Mexico. Seventeen Americans died in the attack, and President Wilson ordered Pershing to conduct a punitive expedition into Mexico to capture Pancho Villa. The full-scale mobilization President Wilson ordered along the Mexican border created a demand for inspectors that had to be satisfied quickly.[134] A major by this time, Conner received his orders detailing him to the Inspector General's office in June 1916 as an inspector of field artillery. His recent service on the border and his familiarity with operations from Laredo to Naco earned him a position working once again for his old boss, Tasker Bliss. Bliss, who was currently serving as Assistant Army Chief of Staff, had been ordered by Secretary of War Baker to tour the Army posts along the border and report back with his impressions. At one point they ventured 150 miles into Mexican territory to visit Pershing's headquarters. Conner experienced a reunion with his friend George Patton who was serving as an aide to Pershing and who personally escorted General Bliss and his party back to Columbus, New Mexico, following their visit.[135]

Chapter Three
Master of His Craft

To War!

Fox returned to the War Department in Washington before Christmas 1916. After spending the holidays with Bug's family in Ossining, he settled into a job working directly for Colonel Andre W. Brewster, the Army's Inspector General. Brewster had distinguished himself during the Boxer Rebellion in China and received the Medal of Honor for his valor. Conner's principal duties involved inspecting units in and around Washington, DC, and helping to compile an annual report on the Regular Army and National Guard Field Artillery units. From this vantage point in the nation's capital he observed America's steady progress towards war.

On June 28, 1914, the Archduke Franz Ferdinand of Austria was assassinated by a Serbian nationalist. This event is often cited as the cause of what was then known as the Great War. In reality, militant nationalism had been building in Europe for decades following the Franco-Prussian War in 1870. Ferdinand's assassination provided a convenient excuse for European powers who were already spoiling for a fight. The Austro-Hungarian empire responded by declaring war on the Kingdom of Serbia. Russia came to Serbia's defense, Germany supported Austria, and by September the conflict had expanded to include France and Britain as well in what we now call World War I.

Germany invaded France using the plans originally developed by Count Alfred von Schlieffen. In response, France executed a defensive strategy known as Plan XVII, the same plan that Conner had studied as an exchange officer to France in 1911. It proved disastrous and the French were routed by the Germans. From the Marne to the Somme, French and British forces sought to repel the Germans on the Western front. Most of their tactics, however, had not changed since the 1870s and did not take into account the vastly more lethal weapons available in 1914. Machine guns, barbed wire, and improved artillery cannons wreaked havoc on troop formations and both sides began to dig in. The era of trench warfare had arrived.

America had no stomach for war. From 1914 until 1917 the nation watched the carnage unfold in Europe while trying to maintain neutrality. "He kept us out of war," was President Woodrow Wilson's campaign slogan as he ran for re-election in 1916. His opponent, Supreme Court Justice Charles Hughes, responded by accusing Wilson of not being sufficiently neutral and called for "strict and honest neutrality."[136] This neutrality, however, came at a cost. In May 1915, a German submarine sank the British passenger liner *RMS Lusitania*, killing 128 American passengers. President Wilson demanded that Germany cease all attacks on passenger ships and, for a time, Germany complied.

In January 1917, however, Germany resumed its policy of unrestricted submarine warfare. Within weeks German U-boats had sunk seven U.S. merchant ships. This outrage was exacerbated by the news that Germany had tried to enlist Mexico's help should the U.S. come to the aid of the Allies with a secret telegram known as the Zimmerman telegram. Germany promised to help Mexico to reclaim New Mexico, Texas, and Arizona in return for a Mexican declaration of war against the United States. President Wilson was outraged. He made the contents of the telegram public and went to Congress asking for action. Congress declared war against the Central Powers on April 6, 1917. Britain and France each sent delegations to Washington to consult with their new ally. The French Foreign Affairs minister, René Viviani, and Marshal Joseph Joffre of the French Army led the French delegation, which arrived in Washington on April 25. One week earlier, Conner received orders to serve as a liaison officer to the French commission.

Conner was uniquely suited for this new assignment. Though he was fluent in French, he was not selected merely for his translating capabilities. His assignments at Fort Riley and the War College had made him the foremost expert in American artillery doctrine. His time with the 22nd Artillery in Versailles meant that he knew more about French military policy, regulations, and protocols than any other officer in the American Army as well. He developed a close relationship with his French counterpart on the commission, Colonel Remond, and with the French liaison to the General Staff, Colonel Edouard Requin. Their friendship and ability to work well together helped the commission to quickly decide matters of organization, supply and strategy as America geared up for war. Excellent work with the commission did not, however, guarantee that Conner would see combat.

President Wilson selected General Pershing to lead the American forces. Pershing had less than a month to select a division staff and outfit them for the trip to Europe, where they would become the nucleus of the American Expeditionary Forces (AEF). He needed a strong chief of staff to organize this massive undertaking. He picked Major James Harbord, an old friend from

Conner (right) and Colonel Remond, French Mission, 1917. [Courtesy of Norm MacDonald]

the Tenth Cavalry, and tasked him to select the rest of the staff. Conner's boss Andre Brewster became the Division Inspector General, and Conner rushed home one afternoon in May to tell Bug that he too would be going to France with Pershing. No doubt Pershing knew of him from his role in the Punitive Expedition, and when Brewster selected him as his artillery expert, both Pershing and Harbord agreed.[137]

After nineteen years in the Army, Conner was a master of his craft. Now he would get to put his knowledge to use. Bug was not happy but she was supportive. She "felt very strongly that Fox, who had devoted his entire life to the study of war, [should] not be left behind. I saw and talked with many officers whose hearts were broken because the War Department could not spare them."[138]

On May 26, 1917, Conner and his wife had dinner at the Patton house in Washington, DC. Ever the politician, Patton had also invited Senator James Phelan of his home state of California.[139] Patton was still serving as one of Pershing's aides, although his name did not appear as such on the official roster creating the American Expeditionary Forces.[140] Instead, Patton would serve as the company commander for the Pershing's headquarters. Two days later he and Conner joined General Pershing's party sailing from New York on the White Star Line's *Baltic*. Although elaborate pains were taken to ensure secrecy, the story was too big to contain. Boxes had been stacked in plain view on Pier 60 for two days, labeled "S.S. *Baltic*, General Pershing's Headquarters."[141]

The trip across the Atlantic was not a vacation. The first morning, General Pershing announced a regular schedule of work for the entire group. A British officer delivered lectures on the British Army and logistical problems. French lessons were carried out in groups at assigned times. Since Conner was

13-GENERAL PERSHING LOOKING FOR SISTER ON NAVAL LAUNCH COMING UP N.Y. HARBOR.

Departing on the **Leviathan***. Conner is center with hat raised. General Pershing is in front of him with binoculars. [Courtesy of Norm*

already fluent in French, he helped out with the lessons. Each of the staff was vaccinated against typhoid and, as they drew closer to the English coast, each took a greater interest in the boat drills.[142] They had good reason, as the *Baltic* had narrowly evaded two torpedoes on its passage to America.[143]

Lieutenant Colonel John Palmer, Conner's co-author on the single promotion list article six years earlier, was in charge of General Pershing's Operations Section. Pershing gave Palmer and his assistant, Major Hugh Drum, a special mission. Pershing wanted them to compile a report on the port facilities of France to prepare for the massive American troop movements that were to come. Though the initial estimate the previous month for the American force was 9,000, Pershing had decided to plan for a force of around one million men. Desperately undermanned, Palmer began to look around for assistance. He didn't have to look farther than his table companions for the voyage.

Palmer was familiar with four of the five officers he dined with on the *Baltic*. He had served with Major Dennis Nolan on the General Staff and Hugh Drum worked for him. Major Arthur Conger had taught Palmer at Fort Leavenworth. He had known Conner since 1911. As Palmer tells it, "Fox Conner was my man; I needed no prolonged period of trial to determine this. I had seen him at work on the General Staff and well knew what substantial abilities he possessed."[144]

Palmer wanted Conner reassigned from the Inspector General's staff to his own Operations Section. He pressed his case with Harbord, who agreed to present the matter to General Pershing. After discussing it with Pershing, Harbord called Palmer to his stateroom later that day and brought up only one objection. The possibility existed that Fox Conner, as a Field Artillery officer, would be promoted before Palmer. If that occurred, Palmer would find himself subordinate to Conner in the Operations Section. Palmer replied, "If that should happen, I would be very glad to change desks with Conner. I recommended him for the job because I believe that nobody else is so well fitted to serve in that capacity and I certainly would not revoke the recommendation even if it should prove prejudicial to my own fortunes."[145] Harbord let him have Conner, a decision that proved itself many times in the years to come.

France

After ten uneventful days at sea, the *Baltic* arrived in Liverpool, England, on June 8, 1917. After an official welcome by the Royal Welsh Fusiliers, the Americans traveled to London by train.[146] Pershing's party spent six days in England getting to know their new allies, attending luncheons, dinners, and briefings. Palmer's operations section spent time at the War Office and began to grasp the vast complexity of moving hundreds of thousands of troops and equipment to the front. Palmer and Conner visited the army training center at Colchester, sixty miles northeast of London. They spent the day watching British soldiers train for trench warfare, examining a bayonet course, gas school, and trench raid.[147]

On June 13, Conner and the staff of the A.E.F. crossed the English channel from Folkestone to Boulogne. Taking a train from Boulogne to Paris, they were greeted by throngs of Parisians shouting "Vive l'Amerique." Several days of celebration followed, with more dinners and ceremonies for Pershing and his senior staff to attend while the lower-ranking officers took time to explore Paris.

To some this might seem like time wasted, with the British and French forces on the continent suffering tremendous losses.

At this point, however, the AEF only had the 190 officers and staff that Pershing had brought in his advance party. Only a century earlier, British forces had captured Washington, DC, and burned the White House to the ground. These early days of receptions and parties allowed the new allies to take each other's measure and gain a trust and respect for each other. Pershing understood that and conducted himself appropriately in every situation, from dinner with King George V in London to a briefing near the front line with French commander Henri Pétain.

On Sunday, June 17, 1917, Pershing and his staff began the monumental task of planning for the American forces currently mobilizing across the Atlantic. They set up a temporary headquarters in a house across from Les Invalides. The most important decision at hand was which section of the front the Americans would occupy, but this decision hinged on interrelated evaluations of suitable ports, railway lines and training areas.[148]

Pershing put together a study group consisting of Hugh Drum, John Palmer, Fox Conner, Major Frank Parker, and Major Sanford H. Wadhams and tasked them with recommending the precise location to fight the enemy.[149] This complex planning mission was difficult but not impossible, because the situation resembled scenarios they had worked through at the School of the Line and the Staff College at Leavenworth, where each of these officers had excelled. Often the scenarios at Leavenworth had used the same maps that they now studied in earnest.[150]

Within a week, the study group made its recommendation. On June 26 General Pershing returned to Pétain's headquarters and requested the Lorraine sector, between the Vosges Mountains and the Argonne Forest. Conner recommended an attack on the German salient at Saint-Mihiel for the American's first offensive. Because they were surrounded on three sides, Conner felt the Germans at Saint-Mihiel were especially vulnerable. A successful strike by the Americans could cut off German access to the rail lines at Metz. It would be over a year, however, before the AEF had the opportunity to put this plan into action. In the meantime, Pershing concentrated on preparing to receive the thousands of troops mobilizing in America.[151]

For his headquarters, Pershing chose the city of Chaumont. This bustling city with a population of 20,000 lay in the upper Marne region of France. Chaumont was a relatively young town by European standards, being only one thousand years old. It is located in the scenic rolling countryside between what were once the feudal kingdoms of Burgundy and Lorraine.[152] By selecting Chaumont as the location for the American Expeditionary Forces' General Headquarters, or AEF GHQ, Pershing took advantage of the town's strategic railroad station.[153]

Promotions happened quickly in the AEF, partly because of relationships with British and French allies. Pershing had no time for protocol if it interfered with productivity, but often the allies would insist on conferring with peers instead of subordinates. An American major might find himself locked out of an important meeting simply because he was not the same rank as the French and British officers in the room. Fox Conner, having sailed to England in May as a Lieutenant Colonel, found himself promoted to Colonel by August.

Pershing was anxious to leave Paris and move closer to the future American sector. On September 1, 1917 Colonel Conner traveled with Patton to set up at the new General Headquarters (GHQ) at Chaumont.[154] The GHQ occupied a four-story barracks building which was formerly the home of a French regiment.[155] The hub of the AEF was a small room on the second floor of the main barrack building measuring 18 feet by 12 feet. A map of the western front dominated one wall. A lone desk sat in the middle of the room, where General John "Black Jack" Pershing would sit to receive updates from his staff. Conner and the others on the staff grew accustomed to long hours, often spending twelve hours a day at their desks, seven days a week with only an occasional Sunday afternoon respite. There was much to be done, since by the end of September there were already more than 61,000 American soldiers in the AEF, training in encampments scattered among the small sleepy villages and towns of the Lorraine valley.[156]

Pershing despised the emphasis by British and French forces on trench warfare, seeing it as a stalemate and not a path to victory. He wanted American troops to focus on open warfare and break through German lines, not be content to sit in trenches and trade artillery barrages. Initially the First Division received training from the French 47th Division, but within months the GHQ had resolved to conduct its own training. The training section of the general staff (G-5) laid out the American strategy for training which consisted of three one-month phases. For the first month in France, units would practice tactics at the small unit level. The second month they would rotate to a quiet sector of the front. In the third month troops would train with divisional assets like artillery and aviation in conducting offensive maneuvers.[157]

The first American battalions to see action occupied their positions in the line on October 21. Two weeks later, on November 2, the First Division of the AEF suffered its first combat fatalities from a German raid at Artois. Company F of the 16th Infantry had eleven soldiers captured and three killed in the raid.[158] Two other developments in November complicated the situation for the Allied powers. Russia withdrew from the war following the

AEF Strategy Map, 1917, duplicated from Pershing's memoirs. [Courtesy of Norm MacDonald]

success of Lenin's Bolshevik revolution. That same month, Italian forces suffered a crushing blow at the hands of the Germans at Caporetto. The Germans resolved to commit additional forces to the Western front in the spring.

Throughout the bitterly cold winter, the Americans continued to train and rotate into the trenches. As a member of the operations staff, Conner frequently visited the front to inspect units and report back to Pershing. These inspections were not without risk and he was wounded in early February. In a letter home to Beatrice, Patton recounts the story in a tone that seems almost envious. "Col. Fox Conner got wounded last week. They were inspecting and came to a part of the trench full of water. They climbed out on the top and ran along to avoid the water when just as they were jumping in again a shell blew up and cut Col. C's nose and throat. He is all right again and will get a wound badge which is nice."[159]

On March 21st the Germans launched Operation Michael, an offensive attack into the valley of the Somme river against Britain's Third and Fifth Armies. The German onslaught overwhelmed British defenses, and General Sir Douglas Haig requested reinforcements. By this time the AEF had swelled to 300,000 soldiers, and General Pershing committed the 1st Division to join the French First Army in coming to the aid of the British. The AEF was on its way to its first major battle of the war in a place called Cantigny. By the time the Americans attacked on May 28, the majority of German forces had moved on to other sectors, leaving only a reserve division to hold the tiny village. Nonetheless, the success of the First Division at Cantigny showed that the AEF could plan and execute division level operations on its own. It also played a role in helping Fox Conner to identify a new protégé. He had already been observing the First Division's

Colonel Conner as G-3 in Chaumont, 1918-1919. [Courtesy of Norm MacDonald]

operations officer for several months, and the success at Cantigny confirmed Conner's intention to bring him to the AEF GHQ. The officer in question was Lieutenant Colonel George C. Marshall.

While General Pershing, shown here on a hunting trip, retired in 1924, he remained in touch with Conner the remainder of his life. [Courtesy of Norm MacDonald]

Chapter Four
Conner and Marshall – A Mutual Admiration Society

July, 1918
Chaumont, France

On Wednesday, July 17, 1918, George C. Marshall reported for duty at Pershing's headquarters in Chaumont around 9 p.m.[160] His new boss was Colonel Fox Conner, chief of the Operations Section.[161] Marshall had attracted Conner's attention while serving as the operations officer for the 1st American Division seven months earlier. Conner believed in walking the ground rather than relying on reports sent back to Chaumont from the division headquarters. It was through one of these observation trips that he heard about Marshall from Major Robert Lewis, a liaison officer to the French Army.[162] Conner arranged to meet Marshall and was very impressed. A busy man himself, Conner began devoting one day each week to working with Marshall at the 1st Division headquarters in Menil-la-Tour.[163] Following the 1st Division's success at Cantigny, Conner had Marshall transferred to the staff at Chaumont.

Conner was not the first man to be impressed by George Marshall. Indeed, each of Conner's three major protégés had formidable talents in their own right prior to their relationship with their mentor. For his part, Marshall was serving as an aide to General Franklin Bell when the first World War began. Marshall desperately wanted to join the American Expeditionary Forces and even interviewed with Pershing as he prepared to sail for France on the recommendation of Pershing's Chief of Staff, James Harbord. In the end, Pershing did not want to deprive Bell of his aide and Marshall had to seek other means to join the AEF. He petitioned General Bell to use his influence and succeeded in joining the 1st Division staff, where he came to Conner's attention.[164]

But for the difference of a few weeks, Marshall and Conner could have met twelve years earlier. Conner graduated from the Staff College at Leavenworth in 1906. The faculty of the College recommended him for a teaching assignment there, but he was assigned to Fort Riley, Kansas as the post adjutant instead.[165] Marshall arrived at Leavenworth to begin his studies at the General Service and Staff College the same summer that Conner left for Fort Riley.[166] Upon his arrival at Chaumont, Marshall learned that he would be sharing a room with Colonel LeRoy Eltinge, the AEF's Deputy Chief of Staff.[167] Conner and Marshall became very close, and the two were often referred to as a "mutual admiration society."[168]

Conner and Marshall began developing plans for the Saint-Mihiel offensive. This offensive through the Lorraine region of France had been on Conner's mind for almost a year. To him, the reinforcement of the British in the Somme and the battle of Belleau Wood fought by the 2nd Division were distractions from the main objective of reducing the German salient at Saint-Mihiel. The area in question was an historic invasion route into France and Conner hoped that a successful attack would threaten to envelop the German line.[169] Conner had brought Marshall to Pershing's staff with this offensive in mind. Marshall's grasp of operational planning and strategy rivaled Conner's, and he appreciated the flexibility of having such a capable subordinate. By this time, Conner was an invaluable asset to Pershing because of his language skills and his familiarity with the both the French Army and the AEF. He often traveled with Pershing and was grateful to have someone with Marshall's capabilities back at Chaumont overseeing the planning of the Saint-Mihiel salient.

A firm believer in competition as a winnowing process, Conner assigned the duty of planning the offensive to both Marshall and Colonel Walter Grant. Each was to work on their individual plans separately and submit them to Conner for review. Selecting Marshall's, he told both men to develop that plan further. Marshall worked tirelessly, revising the plan at least four times over the course of the next few weeks.

On July 24, 1918, General Pershing left Chaumont to attend a meeting with Marshal Foch at his headquarters. He brought Colonel Conner and a few others with him. At this meeting Foch charged Pershing with the mission to reduce the salient at Saint-Mihiel. The offensive operation Conner had envisioned and planned for was approved for execution in September.[170] At the end of the day, Pershing returned to Chaumont and issued a formal order creating the First Army, effective that day, with a headquarters at La Ferte-sous-Jouarre, about 15 miles southwest of Verdun.[171]

Two weeks later Conner was promoted to Brigadier General on August 6. Four days later, the First Army of the American Expeditionary Forces became operational. Tired of administrative battles and diplomatic skirmishes, Pershing longed for action. He made himself commander of the First Army despite Conner's objections to the contrary. Conner vehemently opposed the idea because he felt Pershing's attention would be split between two distinct jobs, each with a separate headquarters. In this instance his objections did not sway Pershing. Ever the obedient staff officer, Conner sought to mitigate what he felt was a poor decision by detailing Marshall to the staff of the First Army. Marshall was promoted to colonel on August 27.[172] As a member of the operations staff for the First Army, he found himself in the unique position of reviewing the plans for the Saint-Mihiel offensive that he had personally written while on the AEF staff at Chaumont.

On August 30, only one more obstacle stood between Pershing's First Army and the battle of Saint-Mihiel. Surprisingly, it was the French Army. More specifically, it was Marshal Foch. He visited Pershing at his Army headquarters and suggested a change. Instead of proceeding with the attack on Saint-Mihiel, why not join the French Second Army in an attack further west, in the Argonne region? As Foch talked, it became increasingly clear to Pershing that he meant to use the American forces not as a single unit but in piecemeal fashion. Having spent over a year creating a distinct American force, Pershing was not about to parse it out as reinforcements for the French. He refused and they exchanged heated words before Foch departed.

Frustrated, Pershing appealed the next day to Pétain, who mediated a compromise during a meeting with both Pershing and Foch on September 2. The Americans could proceed with the attack on Saint-Mihiel, provided they joined the French forces in the Meuse-Argonne offensive before the end of the month. That meant the First Army would conduct two major operations within three weeks' time. It also meant that success at Saint-Mihiel could not be exploited with further movement towards Metz. This seemed like a monumental task and consequently appealed to Pershing's vanity. He agreed, and on September 12, 1918, over 500,000 American troops began the battle of Saint-Mihiel.[173]

The Germans had anticipated an attack on the salient for months and had already begun to withdraw. Seeking an overwhelming victory, Pershing sent twelve divisions of American and French troops against the eight German divisions trying to leave Saint-Mihiel intact. In the end, the AEF captured over 14,000 German prisoners in two days. Like Cantigny however, the Americans found their success to be more significant than their allies. The First Army staff immediately turned to planning for the campaign in the Meuse-Argonne region. The Army chief of staff, General Hugh Drum, tasked Marshall with devising a plan for moving 400,000 men and their equipment from Saint-Mihiel to the Meuse-Argonne, a distance of about 50 miles. Two factors added a level of complexity to his planning. First, there were only three main roads into the designated sector. Second, troops could only travel at night to avoid detection. Conner was undoubtedly impressed with his protégé's performance of this complicated maneuver, balancing the movements of three separate Corps.

The Souilly Memo

On November 5, 1918, Conner visited Marshall's office in Souilly at the First Army headquarters at about four o'clock in the afternoon. According to Marshall's account, they made small talk for about 30 minutes about the conduct of the war and the situation the Germans found themselves in. The Meuse-Argonne campaign, which had commenced on September 26, had effectively broken the German forces and the Americans were in pursuit. In particular, the German-occupied city of Sedan looked particularly vulnerable to the Allies. The Germans had captured the city in 1870 during the Franco-Prussian war, and had repeated that capture in the early days of the current war. Retaking Sedan was a point of pride for the French and on November 4th, Marshal Foch had imposed a new western boundary on the American army. The boundary bent eastward and touched the Meuse River three kilometers below Sedan. This would prevent American forces from taking Sedan. Pershing, however, thought Sedan might be the final battle of the war and wanted that honor for the AEF. With that in mind but with no official orders from Pershing, Conner sought out Marshall at Souilly.

After talking for a half hour together, Conner said, "It is General Pershing's desire that the troops of the First Army should capture Sedan, and he directs that orders be issued accordingly." Marshall called for a stenographer and dictated a memo to issue to the First and Fifth Corps to march into Sedan.[174]

November 5, 1918

Memorandum for Commanding Generals, 1st Corps, 5th Corps.

Subject: Message from Commander-in-Chief.

1. General Pershing desires that the honor of entering Sedan should fall to the First American Army. He has every confidence that the troops of the 1st Corps, assisted on their right by the 5th Corps, will enable him to realize this desire.

2. In transmitting the foregoing message, your attention is invited to the favorable opportunity now existing for pressing our advantage throughout the night.

General Conner told Marshall to issue the order immediately. Marshall laughed and said, "Am I expected to believe that this is General Pershing's order, when I know damn well you came to this conclusion during our conversation?" General Conner insisted that this was an order from the Commander-in-Chief. Marshall was reluctant to issue the order without consulting with General Liggett, the army commander and General Drum, his Chief of Staff, even though he approved of the idea.

Marshall proposed to wait until 6 p.m. and then issue the order if neither Liggett nor Drum returned by then. Conner was not enthusiastic, but agreed. At five minutes to six, General Drum returned to his office. Marshall brought him a copy of the order to review. Drum agreed with the order, but added the line "Boundaries will not be considered binding." Marshall called the order to 1st and 5th Corps around 6:10 p.m. Marshall claimed he found out later that Pershing had given similar instructions at 5 p.m. to General Dickman of First Corps.[175]

These orders created a controversy that lasted well beyond the First World War. The 42nd Division of First Corps raced towards Sedan. At the same time, the 1st Division of Fifth Corps altered its route because of the phrase "boundaries will not be considered binding" and raced towards Sedan as well. The commander of the French Fourth Army wrote a scathing indictment of the American maneuver. It was only by luck that the two American units did not fire on each other as they converged on the medieval fortress town. Douglas MacArthur, who was a brigade commander in the 42nd (Rainbow) Division, was temporarily detained by members of the 16th Infantry when he went forward to discover the identity of the American troops blocking his unit's advance. For years afterward he would talk of the problems caused by the "Chaumont" crew, meaning Pershing, Conner, and Marshall.

Armistice

The war ended at the eleventh hour of November 11, 1918, with Germany's signing of the Armistice agreement. Marshall rejoined Conner on Pershing's staff at the AEF-GHQ at the end of January, 1919. For the next eight months, they had the unenviable task of overseeing the return of almost two million American soldiers and equipment to the United States, while simultaneously preparing various after-action reports on the war overall and special reports on the Saint-Mihiel and Meuse-Argonne offensives.

The Peace Treaty was signed in Versailles on June 28, 1919. Fox Conner accompanied Pershing to the signing ceremony. Later, he confided to Marshall that the terms of the treaty practically guaranteed another war. Together they traveled with Pershing to Waterloo in August. By this time, Marshall had Conner's complete confidence. In much the same way that Palmer and Harbord had lobbied on his behalf to Pershing, Conner now recommended Marshall to Pershing. On September 8, 1919, the *Leviathan* docked at Hoboken, NJ, with General Pershing, General Fox Conner, Colonel Marshall, and Colonel Quekemeyer aboard.[176] Pershing and his staff were honored guests of New York City and enjoyed complimentary lodgings at the Waldorf-Astoria Hotel. Official receptions in Philly and Washington, DC, followed.

General Pershing was called upon by the President and Congress to give his views on the future of the military. Brigadier General Conner helped to form those views. Anticipating the call to testify before Congress, he and Marshall prepped Pershing in Europe throughout the summer of 1919 and continued to work with him throughout the fall after their triumphant return to America.

On October 7, 1919, Pershing met Conner in Utica and proceeded to the Brandreth lake camp. Conner's sister-in-law Paulina and her friend Elsie Robinson provided companionship for Pershing.[177] From October 7th to October 25th, Pershing and Marshall were sequestered at the Brandreth family compound finalizing his testimony on the reorganization of the Army.[178] On October 31, 1919, Pershing appeared before a combined meeting of Senate and House military committees. The testimony lasted three days, with Marshall sitting on one side of Pershing and Conner on the other side.[179] That winter, Conner and Marshall accompanied Pershing on a tour of army installations. Other officers on the trip included George Van Horn Moseley and Malin Craig.[180]

A Lifelong Friendship

Their friendship, forged in the stress and strain of combat, would continue for thirty years. Conner had a very high opinion of George C. Marshall, and he later told Ike that Marshall "knows more about the techniques of arranging allied commands than any man I know. He is nothing short of a genius."[181] For his part, Marshall appreciated the opportunities that working for Conner had created for him. Because of his work with Conner, Marshall became Pershing's aide after the war when Pershing was the Army Chief of Staff. Marshall visited the Conners in Panama in August 1924 and narrowly missed meeting Eisenhower, who had left Panama that summer.[182] A decade later Marshall encouraged Conner to write a book about his experiences in the Great War. Pershing's memoirs had appeared in print a few years earlier, and Marshall felt that they didn't tell the full story of the AEF. When approached by Roger Scaife, the publisher of Little, Brown and Company, about the possibility of a book on the AEF, Marshall

Pershing party at Brandreth, 1920. From left to right: Elsie Robinson, General Pershing, Beatrice Hahn, Bug, Fox, George Marshall. Betty Conner is seated. [Courtesy of Norm MacDonald]

immediately suggested he contact Conner.[183] Conner and Scaife met over lunch and Conner tentatively agreed to write such a book. Ultimately he did not complete it, perhaps because of the admonishment Marshall sent to him when he requested ideas on chapter headings. Although he enthusiastically endorsed Conner as the man for the job, he also warned that such a book would not be "of great interest unless it were a very honest statement of the facts. This would mean that 'many toes would be tread on' and much 'yapping' would result."[184]

Upon Conner's retirement in 1938, Marshall wrote, "I am deeply sorry, both personally and officially, to see you leave the active list, because you have a great deal yet to give the Army out of that wise head of yours. General Pershing was talking about you a few days before he sailed for France, and as always in the most complimentary terms possible regarding your wisdom and judgment."[185]

Chapter Five
Conner and Eisenhower –
Growing a Supreme Commander

October, 1920
Fort Meade, Maryland

On one sunny but cold Saturday, George Patton found himself escorting his old friend and mentor as he inspected the Infantry Tank School at Fort Meade, Maryland. Brigadier General Fox Conner was serving as the Chief of Staff to General Pershing in Washington, DC, and had recently helped Pershing to prepare his Congressional testimony regarding the National Defense Act, which had passed into law four months earlier. Patton had served in Pershing's headquarters at Chaumont and had known Conner since their days at Fort Riley seven years earlier.

As George and Fox walked around the grounds, Bug Conner caught up with Patton's wife Beatrice. They had kept in touch during the war while their husbands were away and had much in common. Both were world travelers from wealthy families. During a break from inspecting the post, Conner mentioned over coffee that he was due to take over command of Camp Gaillard in Panama and needed to find a capable young officer to serve as his executive officer. His time on the Army staff during and after the war had left him out of touch with young officers, so he asked Patton for a recommendation. Only one name came to

Patton's mind, that of his good friend and next door neighbor, Major Dwight David Eisenhower.[186] Intrigued, Conner asked to meet Major Eisenhower, who was known to all of his friends as Ike.

George Patton had graduated from West Point in 1909, six years ahead of Ike. After his return from World War I, Patton began studying for the Command and General Staff College at Fort Leavenworth, Kansas. He invited Ike to help him study, and together they would spend many evenings working out the solutions to problems from previous years' curriculum while their wives chatted.[187] Though Mamie Eisenhower and Beatrice Patton were not close, they remained friendly to each other because of the close friendship their husbands shared. Mamie's only sports interest was watching football, while Bea maintained an interest in sailing, deep-sea fishing and horseback riding. Bea had travelled widely and had many wealthy and influential friends, while Mamie preferred a quieter domestic life. The instant and transient friendship they shared was a common feature of Army wives of the day. They were friends mostly because their husbands were friends and because they were neighbors. The Eisenhowers lived next door to the Pattons and spent long hours fixing up the former barracks building that comprised their duplex. Mamie often found herself scrimping and scraping to fix up their home while Bea Patton would host dinners on fine china next door.[188]

Both Mamie Eisenhower and her husband Ike have often maintained that the dinner the following Sunday afternoon, and the introduction of Ike to Fox Conner at that dinner, was the pivotal moment in determining Ike's future success in the Army.[189] The Pattons were known for their weekly Sunday dinners and followed the tradition of hospitality and social gatherings common in the officer corps at the time.

Conner made no mention of the position in Panama as the three couples ate that Sunday, but he found the young Major Eisenhower very impressive. After dinner, Conner asked Eisenhower and Patton to show him around and give him a tour of their tank training site. Patton slyly took things a step further and offered to give General Conner a ride in a tank. Patton was always trying to stress the advantages of tanks and had even enlisted his wife as a willing passenger on one occasion to impress visiting dignitaries.[190] On hearing this, Bug Conner spoke up and asked to come along. The whippet tanks that Patton was eager to show off only carried two people, so Ike was tasked with driving Bug while Fox rode with Patton. Aware of the dangers inherent in giving tank rides to a civilian, and a general's wife to boot, Ike drove slowly and cautiously but Bug was still rattled by the ride and regretted insisting on it.[191]

After the Conners left, Patton confided to Ike that he had recommended him for the job and encouraged him to take it when it was offered. The fact that Patton had recommended Ike carried great weight with Conner, and a few weeks later a formal offer to Ike arrived in the mail.[192] Ike was moved by his friend's recommendation and excited about the opportunity. He accepted.

Eisenhower had professional and personal reasons to want to leave Fort Meade. After Conner's visit, Ike had written an article for the *Infantry Journal* in which he argued that tanks would be an important force in their own right in future conflicts instead of playing a supporting role to the infantry as they had in World War I. He went so far as to theorize about entire units based around tanks, which could take advantage of their great speed and armor to exploit success on the battlefield, leaving infantry units far behind. Understandably, this kind of writing angered the Infantry Chief, who made it clear that Eisenhower was now *persona non grata* in his own branch. His career in the future would be limited to coaching the Army football team at Fort Meade, an important source of bragging rights during the interwar period.

Personally, the Eisenhowers needed a change of scenery to help soothe the pain brought by the loss of their son Doud. Two months after the Conners' visit, Doud Dwight "Icky" Eisenhower had contracted scarlet fever on December 26, 1920 and passed away one week later. The Eisenhowers were devastated at the loss of their only child, a vibrant and active three-year old. Around every corner at Fort Meade were memories of their Icky, and they saw Panama as a new beginning. Despite their desire to leave for Panama right away, the Chief of the Tank Corps, Brigadier General Samuel Rockenbach, refused to let Ike go because of his success coaching the base football team. It took a personal appeal from Conner to the Infantry Chief, General Charles Farnsworth, to get Ike to Panama. A year after his visit to Fort Meade, Conner wrote to Eisenhower.

October 6, 1921

My Dear Eisenhower,

I enclose copy of the letter I sent the Chief of Infantry on October 4. As you will see I decided it was best not to wait until you could be consulted.

I am more than glad you are willing to come. I hardly expect any great trouble in getting the order. I wrote on the 4ᵗʰ to Col. G.C. Marshall Aide to Gen P. [Pershing] asking him to steer the matter. It might be advisable for you to drop in on Col. Marshall, State War and Navy Building, Room 270, and tell him your desire to go, or, if you can not [sic] get into the city, to telephone him.

Yours,
Fox Conner[193]

Conner's persistence prevailed and in late December 1921, Eisenhower received orders to Panama.[194] He and Mamie joined the Conners at Camp Gaillard on January 7, 1922.[195]

Panama: A Mentorship Begins

The living conditions in the Canal Zone in the 1920s were Spartan at best. Camp Gaillard was named for Colonel David Gaillard, a West Point graduate of the Class of 1884 and the chief engineer of the Panama excavation. The Camp sat on the edge of the Culebra Cut of the Canal, a portion of the passage that was defined largely by mudslides. Ike's granddaughter Susan writes of Camp Gaillard that "tons of land often fell into the canal, which would then have to be dredged, while mudslides interrupted traffic and undermined the stability of the locality."[196]

"A double-decked shanty, only twice as disreputable," was how Mamie described her first impression of their quarters in Panama.[197] The two-story house on stilts was at least twenty years old and had not been occupied in the previous decade. The wooden walls and roof of the shack were rotting and full of holes which let in the seasonal rains. On top of that, the quarters were infested with tropical insects and bats. One of Mamie Eisenhower's first impressions of Camp Gaillard was the rat that gnawed on the leg of a chair in her house all night on that first night.[198] The local area was crawling with snakes and lizards.[199]

Mamie might not have even set foot in the house but for

Fox and Old Bill, circa 1922. [Courtesy of Norm MacDonald]

the quick actions of Bug Conner. The general's wife saw the dismay in the Eisenhowers' faces upon their arrival and rapidly escorted them to her own quarters less than a hundred yards away. A point of particular interest to Mamie was the piano in the Conners' living room. Bug invited Mamie to avail herself of the piano during their stay in Panama. Bug herself played the violin, and the two of them would often provide music for church services on Sundays. After seeing how a little paint and hard work had transformed the Conner quarters into something passable, Mamie and Ike were less discouraged about their new assignment.[200]

As with each of his protégés, Conner saw an aspect of his own personality in Ike. Both of them had grown up far from the politically and culturally sophisticated East Coast Establishment, on farms in rural America. Like Conner, Eisenhower had graduated in the middle of his class at West Point, ranking 61st out of 164 classmates. As a couple with three children of their own, the Conners took a special interest in the young Eisenhowers and were sensitive to their recent loss.

Fox Conner took Ike under his wing. Both avid horsemen, they would take long rides through the jungle together and fish on the weekends. It was not unusual for them to spend eight hours a day on horseback inspecting the camp and the canal. Conner's brigade, the 20th Infantry, was a Puerto Rican regiment. Although the officers were mostly Caucasian, the enlisted men and sergeants were all Puerto Rican. This was partly due to American attitudes about segregation at the time, and partly out of the mistaken belief that "brown" people do better in tropical climates because it more closely approximated their native island. There is no record of overt discrimination by Conner or Ike. Though both seemed to accept the segregated aspect of the Army at the time, both were seen as caring and effective leaders who sought to ensure a decent quality of life for the soldiers under their care. There were weekly dances at the camp club and a swimming pool. On clear, hot nights movies were projected on an outdoor screen.[201]

For her part, Bug Conner took Mamie aside and helped her to cope with both the loss of Doud and the resulting emotional distance with Ike. In her memoirs Bug says she advised Mamie to "vamp him." A mature mother of three children who'd been married twenty years, Virginia wanted the young couple to succeed. Her advice worked. Mamie cut her hair and turned her feminine wiles on Ike. She joined the other wives in daily shopping excursions to buy fresh produce from a barge on the canal. She walked across the rickety cat-walk spanning the canal lock gates to Panama City to barter with local merchants for candlesticks, furniture, and silks.[202] She worked with Bug to establish a maternity hospital for the wives of the enlisted men on the camp, raising money with the serendipitous help of a pair of movie stars.

When Mamie heard that Lila Lee and Thomas Meighan were in Panama filming a movie, she hurried down to the Tivoli Hotel and invited them to Camp Gaillard.[203] Lee and Meighan, two of the few silent film stars who would later make the successful transition to "talkies," graciously agreed to bring a copy of their latest movie, *The Ne'er Do Well*, and give the camp an advance screening in addition to being the guests of honor at a fundraising dinner for the maternity ward.

General Conner was not satisfied with Eisenhower's disdain for military history, a product of the methodology in use at the time for teaching it at West Point. In those days, students were forced to memorize the positions of units and their commanders at all points throughout a battle. This amounted to learning of a sort, but did nothing to explain why decisions had been made or how those decisions affected the outcomes of the battles themselves. Conner recalled how he had struggled as a cadet, and how his first regimental commander, Colonel Haskin, had revived his interest in military history and strategy. He resolved to follow the same strategy with Ike, using the vast library in his quarters as his training aid.

Conner's quarters in Panama were filled with books on military history and strategy from floor to ceiling. Half of the volumes were in French. In the first two decades of the twentieth century, far more was written about the study of war on the European continent than in America. Conner had started studying French and Spanish as a cadet, but taught himself German as a captain in order to read about strategies being created in the Prussian *Kriegsakademie*. He began a deliberate campaign to turn his executive officer into a military history aficionado like himself.

He started Eisenhower on military fiction, handing him interesting books to read that they would then discuss. Over time, as Ike's interest in the subject grew, Conner shifted the selections to more serious works. His assignments were eclectic, ranging from Shakespeare to Nietzsche, with Matthew Steele's *American Campaigns* thrown in.[204] Steele's work, the authoritative volume on the Civil War at the time, had first appeared in print 1909 but Conner was familiar with it from the detailed notes he took of Steele's lectures at the Staff College in 1905.[205] After a long day's work Conner and Ike would read biographies of Civil War generals and spent hours discussing their decisions together. Frequently their conversations would continue after dinner long into the night. Conner assigned the writings of the Prussian theorist Carl von Clausewitz, still a military staple, on three separate occasions. Each time he would question Ike about the meanings and conclusions of Clausewitz's seminal work, *On War*.

Conner would often talk about the signing ceremony of the Treaty of Versailles. According to both Bug and Ike, Conner was convinced that the structure of the treaty ending World War I all but guaranteed another war. He theorized that it would happen within a quarter century, and he presciently understood that the next war would be fought, as the last one had been, with allies. Having seen firsthand the difficulties that allied warfare posed in his time on Pershing's staff, Conner was determined to pass on the lessons he had learned.

He urged Eisenhower to learn everything he could about fighting as an allied force, and he even suggested another man from whom to learn it. George C. Marshall, Conner said, "knows more about the techniques of arranging allied commands than any man I know. He is nothing short of a genius."[206] Conner believed that the next war would truly be a world war, and that the men who fought it would have to think in terms of world strategy rather than single-front strategy.[207] Another thing Conner taught Eisenhower was never to have a personal enemy on his staff, since he would sabotage his commander.[208] In 1924, when his time as Conner's executive officer came to a close, Conner wrote on Eisenhower's efficiency report in that he was "one of the most capable, efficient, and loyal officers I have ever met."[209]

A Timely Intervention

Eisenhower left Panama motivated and enthusiastic about his chosen profession, but orders to return to Fort Meade disheartened him. He sought a coveted slot at the Army's Command and General Staff College at Fort Leavenworth, Kansas, but instead found himself coaching the army football team again. Conner knew that attendance at the Command and General Staff College

Army Captain Dwight Eisenhower with Renault FT-17 tank. [Courtesy of Norm MacDonald]

was a necessary step for Ike's career, but the old animosity of the Chief of Infantry towards Ike seemed to make it unlikely that he would ever get a slot. Attendance at the Infantry School at Fort Benning was a prerequisite for Leavenworth, and General Farnsworth seemed determined to prevent Ike from attending either school. Conner decided to use his connections to intervene on Ike's behalf.

He sent Eisenhower a telegram with instructions that, whatever happened next, he was to trust Conner. Next, Conner called on his friend and classmate, Major General Robert Davis. Robert "Corkey" Davis and Conner knew each other as classmates and as colleagues, having served together on Pershing's staff during the war. Davis was Pershing's Adjutant General, or G-1, while Conner had served as the chief operations officer, or G-3. In 1922, Davis became the Adjutant General of the Army, the officer in charge of all personnel actions. Ike soon found himself transferred from Infantry Branch to the Adjutant General's department and assigned to recruiting duty at Fort Logan, Colorado. The Adjutant General's Corps at that time had two slots at Leavenworth each year and, as a favor to Conner, Davis gave one of them to Ike.

When he learned of the plan, Eisenhower expressed concern about his ability to success at Leavenworth because he had not attended the Infantry School at Fort Benning, Georgia. Conner's response was meant to reassure.

> You quit worrying. You are better prepared for Leavenworth than any other man that has graduated from Benning because you have had to do the work required at Leavenworth. I know; I've been through that school, I've been an instructor there. You just go on and keep still when an order comes putting you on recruiting duty. Accept it and don't kick.[210]

The work he referred to was Conner's habit of making Ike write a daily order for the operations of Camp Gaillard. Eisenhower later attributed much of his success at Fort Leavenworth to this practice. When Eisenhower graduated first in his class in 1926, Conner sent a congratulatory message to his protégé.[211] He then arranged to have Ike transferred back to the Infantry Branch, thus circumventing Farnsworth once again. Graduating first at Leavenworth had the effect of marking a man for future distinction, and Ike's performance at Leavenworth attracted the attention of men like General Douglas MacArthur and General Mark Clark. General Clark recommended Ike to Marshall for the War Plans Division in 1941, and it was from this position that he left to take command of the European theater of operations.

The Mentorship Continues

Conner and Ike continued corresponding on matters both personal and professional for over two decades. In a letter from September 1934, Ike commented on the General's habit of spending the fall at Brandreth camp. "It must be about time for you to start your annual pilgrimage to the Adirondacks to bring down a buck. I don't think you have ever reported a complete failure on one of those expeditions, but I have my suspicions that some of the buck you shoot are possibly the kind without horns. Anyway I hope you have fine weather and good hunting."[212]

He wrote to Conner throughout his time as Supreme Allied Commander, sharing his concerns and frustrations. On July 4, 1942, Ike wrote that "more and more in the last few days my mind has turned back to you and to the days when I was privileged to serve intimately under your wise counsel and leadership. I cannot tell you how much I would appreciate, at this moment, an opportunity for an hour's discussion with you on problems that constantly beset me."[213]

Ever the mentor, Conner offered wise counsel in return. He advised Ike to "relieve the pressure on Russia," and all else would follow. He sought to encourage him by writing that "your present detail was, and is, widely approved. No better choice could have been made." Conner closed his letter "with all best wishes and great pride in you. As always yours, Fox Conner."[214]

Ike would go on to become President of Columbia University in 1948 and President of the United States in 1952. He met distinguished leaders from all over the world, but he would often describe Fox Conner as "the ablest man I ever knew."[215]

Chapter Six
Conner and Patton – Unleashing the Tanker

An Early Friendship

The story of the relationship between Patton and Conner, at least the early years of it, has already been told. Of his three famous protégés, Fox Conner had known George Patton the longest. From their first meeting in 1913 on that train rocking its way to Fort Riley, Kansas, they bonded over their common interests. Both loved horses, the Army, and their country. Their wives became fast friends as well who also had a lot in common. Bug and Beatrice both came from wealthy families. Beatrice's father, Frederick Ayer, was a contemporary of Bug's grandfather and was also in the patent medicine business.[216] The Pattons and the Conners enjoyed many weekends and vacations together.

Conner's relationship with Patton resembled that of an older brother. He did not have to ignite a passion in Patton for studying strategy as he had with Ike. Likewise, he did not expect the same level of intellectual discussion that he shared with Marshall. Patton was not a scholar, though he did have a piercing intellect. He was not a coalition builder, as Ike grew to be. Patton was a warrior, pure and simple. Conner recognized that in his character and sought to develop and hone that warrior spirit. The trick with Patton would not be urging him forward, it would be holding him back from damaging his own career.

Though their time together at Fort Riley was brief, Patton and Conner would keep in touch and occasionally their paths would cross before they worked together at Chaumont in 1917. Conner left the border excursions for Fort Sill as Patton was joining Black Jack Pershing's staff as an aide. Conner saw him when he inspected Pershing's headquarters with General Tasker Bliss in August 1916, and Patton volunteered to escort Bliss and Conner back to Columbus, New Mexico.[217] They had dinner together before boarding the *Baltic* as part of Pershing's American Expeditionary Forces. And they spent a lot of time together in Chaumont, where Patton served as the company commander for Pershing's headquarters and his occasional aide. Perhaps Conner's greatest contribution to Patton's career was introducing him to a new invention called the tank.

Tanks

A British colonel named Ernest Swinton first conceived of an armored vehicle to break the stalemate of trench warfare. He was inspired in 1914 by the sight of American caterpillar tractors, the same type of tractors that Conner had inspected for the American Army that year. The first British tank, known as the Mark I, saw action in the Battle of the Somme in September 1916. By the time the Americans declared war, both the British and the French had tanks. Before the AEF headquarters moved from Paris to Chaumont, Conner directed Patton's attention to this new war machine. As Patton wrote in his diary,

> One hot July day in 1917 I was drowsing over the desk of the Concierge at GHQ in Paris (at that time I was holding this high office on the staff). Suddenly my slumbers were disturbed by

an orderly who told me to report to the Operations Officer. There was a certain Major. . . [Fox Conner] introduced me to a French Officer and directed me to listen to his story and report my conclusions. This Frenchman was a Tank enthusiast who regaled me for several hours with lurid tales of the value of his pet hobby as a certain means of winning the war. In the report I submitted. . . I said, couching my remarks in the euphemistic jargon appropriate to official correspondence, that the Frenchman was crazy and the Tank not worth a damn.[218]

Like Conner, Pershing found the idea of an armored vehicle intriguing. The AEF study group he created to investigate the idea of an American tank force recommended the immediate creation of a Tank Department, and a plan to procure 2,200 tanks modeled on both British and French designs. Pershing appointed Lieutenant Colonel LeRoy Eltinge from his operations section as the head of a newly formed Tank Department. In October, Patton was hospitalized for jaundice. He found himself sharing a room with Fox Conner, and their conversation turned to tanks.[219] The next day, Eltinge visited and offered Patton the chance to command the Tank School being created in the town of Langres. After talking to Conner, Patton accepted the job.[220] He departed Chaumont the next month to form the AEF Tank Corps. In March 1917, two months before he sailed on the *Baltic*, Patton had passed his examination for promotion to captain. One year later in April 1918, he was promoted to lieutenant colonel and was poised to make a name for himself in the battles of Saint-Mihiel and Meuse-Argonne. By the end of the year, though he was only 32 years old, Patton was a colonel with a Distinguished Service Cross for valor in battle. He had worked hard and been lucky, but he also owed a debt to the man who had first whispered "tanks" in his ear – Fox Conner.

General "George" Patton and his 320-pound Jew Fish. [Courtesy of Norm MacDonald]

Hawaii

A decade would pass before Patton would find himself working with Conner again. They kept in touch during that time, and Patton introduced Conner to Ike as has already been noted. They wrote to each other often, Conner observed the Sled Machine Gun Mount Patton had invented and recommended it to the War Department for testing.[221] On January 25, 1928, Major General Fox Conner assumed command of the Hawaiian Division and Hawaiian Department, Hawaii.[222] Patton was the Division Intelligence Officer, or G-2. His assignment as G-2 was a punishment, and a step down from his former position as the Division Operations Officer, or G-3. The cause for the punishment was Patton's outspoken nature.

In November 1926 Patton became the G-3 of the Hawaiian Division. As the G-3 he was responsible for all aspects of training and operations within the division. Though equal in rank to the heads of other division staff sections, the G-3 is often seen as first among equals. Patton's habit of speaking his mind showed itself in several incidents where he wrote scathing reviews of training by subordinate units, earning the fury of brigade commanders and senior staff officers alike. Many felt that Patton, reduced after the war back to the rank of major, had crossed a line in his criticism of colonels and brigadier generals. The Division Commander, Major General William Smith, sought to defuse the situation by reassigning Patton. He was consequently moved from G-3 to G-2.

This dismissal infuriated Patton. Fortunately for him, his new commander was his old friend and mentor General Conner. Conner assuaged Patton's feelings somewhat with his comments on Patton's last evaluation in Hawaii. Colonel Francis Cooke, the Division Chief of Staff, rated Patton. Conner's endorsement of the evaluation reads "I concur in the above report. I have known him for fifteen years, in both peace and war. I know of no one whom I would prefer to have as a subordinate commander."[223]

Conner retired in 1938, before the start of World War II, but he kept in touch with Patton throughout the war. Patton would write to him at Brandreth to update him on the status of the war.

Chapter Seven
Conclusion

A Lifetime of Service

Most accounts of Major General Fox Conner end with his mentorship of Eisenhower in the 1920s. For another twenty years, however, Conner would go on to render more service to his country and mentor more aspiring subordinates. He continued to cultivate his friendships with Marshall, Patton, and Ike, and each of these three men held a special place in their hearts for their old boss. Though in time each of them would come to outrank Conner, in each of these three households he was referred to simply as "the General," with no further explanation necessary as to which general one was referencing.[224] In one famous incident, President Franklin Roosevelt attempted to call General Marshall by his first name and was rebuffed. Conner, however, could and did address the future Secretary of State as simply "George." He was one of only a handful of people outside Marshall's immediate family who could get away with that level of familiarity.

Conner served in both staff and command positions following his assignment in Panama. He served as the Assistant Chief of Staff for Supply (G-4) from 1924 to 1926, a job which he hated because it put him back in the political world of Washington. He was permanently promoted to Major General on October 20, 1925 and six months later was appointed Deputy Chief of

Staff of the Army.[225] His replacement as Deputy Chief of Staff was Charles Summerall. Bug notes in her memoirs that Conner and Summerall were "fundamentally uncongenial" towards one another, and Conner wasted no time in leaving Washington as quickly as possible.[226] The Conners left DC in the spring of 1927 but were not due to report to Hawaii for eight months. To pass the time, Conner accepted command of the Army's First Division, and thus came full circle in his career with a command ceremony in May on Governor's Island in New York City.[227] That thought must have crossed his mind as he attended his son's graduation from West Point one month later.[228]

After his time in Hawaii, Conner accepted command of the First Corps Area in October 1930 and moved to his new headquarters in Cambridge, Massachusetts.[229] Three years later, in the midst of the Great Depression, President Roosevelt assigned him the task of supervising the New England Civilian Conservation Corps, and he spent four years overseeing the mobilization of young men into 125 Civilian Corp Companies.

Even Conner, however, could not escape the ravages of time. A lifelong smoker, Conner suffered frequently from illness in his later years. While recovering from an operation in the spring of 1938 he developed coronary thrombosis. Hospitalized in Walter Reed, his room was across the hall from his old boss and friend Black Jack Pershing. Conner accepted that his physical condition would not allow him to continue in the profession he loved, and he departed the Army on terminal leave on July 13, 1938.[230] In the year of Conner's retirement, Pershing told him, "I could have spared any other man in the A.E.F. better than you."[231]

Fox and Bug at Brandreth, circa 1948. [Courtesy of Norm MacDonald]

Fort Shafter, March 19, 1930. Left to Right: LTG Hunter Liggett, Fox Conner, Lt. Trimble Brown (Conner's aide-de-camp). [Courtesy of Norm MacDonald]

An Active Retirement

When his health permitted, Conner still sought to serve the Army. The clouds of war gathering over Europe seemed to validate the concerns he had in Paris in 1919. He continued to write and speak on the subject of his expertise – war. Eight months after his retirement, he gave a lecture at the Army War College as he had every year since 1934. During the height of World War II, classified couriers journeyed to his Brandreth camp with bulging envelopes full of war plans for his review, sent by both Marshall and Eisenhower. The old master looked over maps and orders with names like OVERLORD and TORCH and made copious notes before sending them back to their authors. His star pupils, who were now masters of war in their own right, could not pass up the opportunity to ask his advice or to respond to a request for a personal favor.

Ike's son, John S.D. Eisenhower, visited Conner in December 1943 and reported to his father that "the General" seemed subdued and weakened from a series of strokes.[232] His condition continued to deteriorate. He would live to see the end of the war and to see Ike become president of Columbia University, but not President of the United States. Conner passed away on October 13, 1951, at the age of 77 at Walter Reed Hospital. The memorial service held at the hospital chapel was small and inconspicuous. The only VIP in attendance was recently retired Secretary of State George C. Marshall, who stood by Bug's side and honored his friend and mentor. Conner's family carried his ashes to Brandreth Lake. A few newspapers carried his obituary, but he was mostly forgotten even in his own time. The model he followed for developing strategic leaders, however, would live on. Each of his protégés developed subordinates of their own who would go on to face new challenges during the Cold War, fighting once

Bug Conner returning from Alaska, September 1933. [Courtesy of Norm MacDonald]

again in distant lands like Korea and Vietnam. Today it is time for a new generation of leaders to learn from and follow Conner's example, and to mentor future members of the profession of arms to lead the Army in the twenty-first century.

Fox Conner at Brandreth, circa 1949. [Courtesy of Norm MacDonald]

Notes

1 Louise Ligon, "Biographical Sketch of General Fox Connor," *The Monitor-Herald*, Calhoun City, MS March 12, 1936, 2.

2 Ken Nail, *A History of Calhoun County*. Calhoun County School District, 1975, 82.

3 United State Congress. "Andrew Fuller Fox," *Biographical Directory*. http:/bioguide.congress.gov/scripts/biodisplay.pl?index=F000330.

4 Ligon.

5 Nail, 82.

6 Ligon.

7 Theodore Crackel, *West Point: A Bicentennial History*. Lawrence, KS: University Press of Kansas, 2002, 87-115.

8 *Biographical Directory of the United States Congress.*

9 USMA, *Circumstances of the Parents of Cadets*. Vol. 2 1880-1910.

10 Edward Coffman, *The Old Army*. New York: Oxford University Press, 1986, 223.

11 USMA, *School History of Candidates*. Vol. 1 1880-1899.

12 Crackel, 5, 12, 29. When the Continental Congress disbanded the Army in 1784, twenty-five officers and men remained at Fort Pitt and fifty-five remained at West Point.

13 Sidney Forman, "Why the United States Military Academy was Established in 1802," *Military Affairs*, Vol. 29, No. 1, (Spring 1965), 16-28.

14 George Washington, *The Papers of George Washington: Retirement Series*. Vol. 4, 454-455.

15 Fox Conner, letter dated June 16, 1894. Mississippi State Archives.

[16] Susan Linnerud, *Register of Graduates*. West Point, NY: Association of Graduates, United States Military Academy.

[17] Crackel, 131.

[18] Ibid., 132.

[19] Ibid., 135.

[20] James Kershner, *Sylvanus Thayer – A Biography*, New York: Arno Press, 1982, 329.

[21] Fox Conner, letter dated June 16, 1894. Mississippi State Archives.

[22] Guy V. Henry, Jr., *Life of Guy Henry*. USMA archives, 20.

[23] Fox Conner, letter dated June 16, 1894. Mississippi State Archives.

[24] Ibid.

[25] Linnerud.

[26] Crackel, 87-88.

[27] Henry, 20.

[28] USMA, *Academy Staff Records*. No. 15, June 21, 1894-Dec 31, 1897.

[29] USMA, *Post Orders*. Vol. 14.

[30] Fox Conner, letter dated September 6, 1896. Mississippi State Archives.

[31] Fox Conner, letter dated March 4, 1896. Mississippi State Archives.

[32] Ibid.

[33] USMA, *Academy Staff Records*. No. 15, June 21, 1894-Dec 31, 1897. Plebe fall: Conner ranked 20th in math out of 86. He ranked 43rd in English out of 93. Overall, 24th in the class. Plebe spring: Conner ranked 19th in Math out of 74. He ranked 38th in French out of 76. Overall, 31st in the class. Yearling fall: Conner ranked 23rd in Math (analytical geometry) of 64. He ranked 34th out of 73 in French. He ranked 57th in Drawing of 69. Yearling spring: Conner ranked 21st of 67 in

Math (descriptive geometry). He ranked 35th in French of 68. He ranked 46th of 68 in Spanish. He was 31st overall of 65. Cow fall: Conner ranked 7th in philosophy of 64. He ranked 16th of 61 in Chemistry. He ranked 18th of 65 in Drill and Regs (Artillery and Infantry). He ranked 54th in Drawing of 65. Cow spring: Conner ranked 9th in philosophy of 59. He ranked 12th in Chemistry. He ranked 46th in Drawing. He ranked 14th overall in the class. Firstie fall: Conner ranked 12th in Engineering. He ranked 21st in Law. He ranked 21st in Ordnance and Gunnery and 20th in History.

[34] USMA, *Report of Delinquencies.* No. 32.

[35] Fox Conner, letter dated January 17, 1897. Mississippi State Archives.

[36] Fox Conner, letter dated January 24, 1897. Mississippi State Archives.

[37] Linnerud.

[38] Otto Hein, *Memories of Long Ago.* New York: Putnam, 1925, 263.

[39] Frank Vandiver, *Blackjack: The Life and Times of John J. Pershing.* Vol. I. College Station, TX: Texas A&M University Press, 1977, 169.

[40] Fox Conner, letter dated December 5, 1897. Mississippi State Archives.

[41] Henry, 20.

[42] USMA, *Post Orders.* Vol. 14.

[43] Vandiver, 171.

[44] 1898 Howitzer, 124.

[45] 1898 Howitzer, 18.

[46] Fox Conner, letter dated August 9, 1897. Mississippi State Archives.

[47] USMA Treasurer's Office, Statement of Payments. July 1, 1894-November 1, 1897.

[48] USMA, *Academy Staff Records.* No. 15, June 21, 1894-Dec 31, 1897.

[49] Henry, 20.

[50] USMA, Post Orders. Vol. 14.

[51] Paul W. Child, ed. *1990 Register of Graduates and Former Cadets 1802-1990.* West Point, NY: Association of Graduates, United States Military Academy, 1990, 319.

[52] USMA Treasurer's Office, Statement of Payments. July 1, 1894-November 1, 1897.

[53] USMA, *Academy Staff Records.* No. 15, June 21, 1894-Dec 31, 1897.

[54] Ibid.

[55] Guy V. Henry, Jr., *Life of Guy Henry.* USMA archives, 20.

[56] Roger J. Spiller, ed. *Dictionary of American Military Biography.* Vol. I. Westport, CT: Greenwood Press, 1984, 198.

[57] W. L. Haskin to the Adjutant General, May 25, 1898. AGO File 76804.

[58] William L. Haskin, *The History of the First Regiment of Artillery.* B. Thurston and Company, 1879.

[59] William Ganoe, *The History of the United States Army.* New York: D. Appleton-Century, 1942. 375-376. During the war, more than a dozen camps were established for the assembly, training and supply of troops, especially, the volunteers who enlisted to fight in the war.

[60] Grimes, George S. *After action report to the Adjutant Light Artillery Battalion,* July 17, 1898, contained in the appendix of "The Artillery At Santiago", by S. D. Parkhurst.

[61] William F. Aldrich, "Fox Conner." *Study Project, U.S. Army War College.* May 1993, 5.

[62] Spiller, 198.

[63] Special Orders, No. 24 dated May 31, 1900. AGO File 76804, Item 324422.

[64] AGO File 76804. Item 330641.

[65] Virginia Conner, *What Father Forbad.* Dorrance, 1951. 71.

[66] Alfred Donaldson, *A History of the Adirondacks.* New York: Century Company, 1921, 60.

[67] *The Republican,* May 23, 1889.

[68] Virginia Conner, 11-12.

[69] Ibid., 17.

[70] Ibid.

[71] *New York Times,* January 26, 1901.

[72] *New York Times,* March 10, 1901.

[73] Virginia Conner, 18-20.

[74] Spiller, 198.

[75] *New York Times,* May 19, 1901. Colonel Francis Moore, 11th Cavalry, served as president of the board. Other board members included Major William B. Davis, Surgeon; Major Earl D. Thomas, Inspector General; Major Peter Leary, Jr., Artillery Corps; and First Lieutenant Jere B. Clayton, Assistant Surgeon.

[76] *New York Times,* May 30, 1901.

[77] AGO File 76804. Report of the "Proceedings of a Board of Officers" dated June 13, 1901.

[78] Virginia Conner, 21.

[79] Spiller, 198.

[80] Phone interview by the author with Reverend Canon Charles P. Pridemore of Trinity Episcopal Church, Ossinging, NY on November 17, 2009.

[81] "Funeral of Dr. Brandreth, Sing Sing Village in Mourning," *New York Times,* February 23, 1880, 8.

[82] *New York Times,* June 5, 1902, 9.

[83] Virginia Conner, 21.

[84] AOG Register 1990.

[85] Harry Ball, *Of Responsible Command; The History of the U.S. Army War College,* Carlisle Barracks, PA: U.S. Army War College, 30.

[86] Ball, 90.

[87] *Staff College Commandant's Annual Report 1905-1906.* Appendix I, 1.

[88] Ibid, 4. The other students admitted were Captains James A. Woodruff, Walter T. Bates, and First Lieutenant Gilbert A. Youngberg.

[89] Ibid, 35. Coffman notes in *The Regulars* that Bell was promoted directly from captain to brigadier general on page 178.

[90] Virginia Conner, 24.

[91] Spiller, 199.

[92] Ibid., 199.

[93] Virginia Conner, 60.

[94] Boyd Dastrup, *King of Battle: A Branch History of the U.S. Army's Field Artillery.* U.S. Army Training and Doctrine Command, 1992, 152.

[95] Theodore Wint, *Souvenir of Maneuver Camp. Fourth Regiment Infantry. South Dakota National Guard.* August 17-28, 1906. M. C. Sessions & Sons. Sioux Falls, South Dakota.

[96] Virginia Conner, 24-25. Also in the Brandreth Guest Book, July 15, 1907, stored at the Ossining Historical Society.

[97] AGO Document File 76804.

[98] Ball, 79.

[99] Ibid., 86.

[100] *New York Times,* "Biggest War Game Ever Played Here," August 11, 1909.

[101] AGO Document File 76804, Item 1559272, dated August 26, 1909.

[102] Irving B. Holley Jr., *General John M. Palmer: Citizen Soldiers and the Army of a Democracy.* West Port, CT: Greenwood Press, 1982, 201.

[103] Holley, 201.

[104] Virginia Conner, 26.

[105] Ibid, 26-27.

[106] Ibid.

[107] Ibid, 28-37.

[108] Ibid, 39.

[109] Ibid.

[110] Ibid, 35.

[111] Ibid, 40.

[112] Fox Conner, "Notes on Lost Motion and Jump." *The Field Artillery Journal.* Volume V. 1915, 536.

[113] In August 1914, the German Army possessed about 3,500 105mm and 155mm howitzers, and France had about 300.

[114] Barbara Tuchman, *The Guns of August.* Random House, 2004, 207.

[115] Oliver Spaulding. *Notes on Field Artillery for Officers of All Arms.* U.S. Cavalry Association, 1914, 78-79.

[116] Tuchman, 207.

[117] Fox Conner, "The Genius of the French Army", *Army Ordnance,* May-June 1934, 328

[118] Tuchman, 28-33.

[119] Ball, 130.

[120] Ganoe, 445.

[121] Spiller, 200.

[122] AGO File 76804. Items 2016757 and 2052501.

[123] AGO File 76804. Item 2128951.

[124] Headquarters, Sixth Field Artillery, U.S.A. *History of the Sixth Field Artillery, 1798-1932,* 140.

[125] Leon Metz, *Desert Army: Fort Bliss on the Texas Border.* Mangan Books, 1995, 82-85.

[126] Virginia Conner, 54-55.

[127] Ibid., 55.

[128] Ibid., 55.

[129] Lucian Truscott, *The Twighlight of the U.S. Cavalry; Life in the Old Army, 1917-1942.* Lawrence, KS: University Press of Kansas, 1989, 2.

[130] Virginia Conner, 56.

[131] Wes Patience, *Bootlegging on the Border.* Audio file, 2006. Cochise College Library.

[132] AGO File 76804. Item 2248237. Dated January 11, 1915.

[133] Virginia Conner, 71.

[134] Joseph Whitehorne, *The Inspectors General of the United States Army 1903-1939.* Washington, DC: Office of the Inspector General, U.S. Army, 31-32.

[135] Martin Blumenson, *The Patton Papers: 1885-1940.* Austin, TX: University of Texas, 1972, 349.

[136] William Degregorio, *The Complete Book of U.S. Presidents.* Fifth edition, New York: Wings Books, 1997, 417-418.

[137] Whitehorne, Joseph W. A., 116.

[138] Virginia Conner, 79.

[139] Blumenson, 389.

[140] General Order No. 1, AEF, May 26, 1917.

[141] Vandiver, vol. II, 698. See also Edward Coffman, *The War to End All Wars.* New York: Oxford University Press, 1968, 122.

[142] Coffman, *The War to End All Wars,* 123.

[143] Harbord, 7.

[144] Holley, 278.

[145] Ibid., 278.

[146] Coffman, 123.

[147] Holley, 282.

[148] Coffman, 125.

[149] Vandiver, vol. II, 730.

[150] Coffman, 125.

[151] Ibid., 125-126.

[152] Harbord, 139.

[153] Ibid., 163.

[154] Blumenson, 415.

[155] Coffman, 131.

[156] Ibid.

[157] Ibid., 138.

[158] Ibid., 140.

[159] Blumenson, 485.

[160] Forest Pogue, *George C. Marshall: Education of a General.* New York: Viking Press, 1963, 169.

[161] Pogue, 169.

[162] Payne, 69.

[163] Frye, 147-148.

[164] Pogue, vol. I, 142.

[165] Spiller, 199.

[166] Pogue, vol. I, 93-94.

[167] Marshall, George C., *Memoirs of My Services in the World War 1917-1918,* 120-121.

[168] Marshall, 120.

[169] Pogue, vol. I, 170.

[170] Coffman, 263-264.

[171] John S.D. Eisenhower. *Yanks: The Epic Story of the American Army in World War I,* 173.

[172] Pogue, vol. I, 172.

[173] Vandiver, vol. II, 936-939. See also Edward Lengel, *To Conquer Hell.* New York: Holt Books 2008, 50-52.

[174] Vandiver, vol. II, 984.

175 Marshall, 189-191.

176 Ibid., Photo inset.

177 Vandiver, vol. II, 1045.

178 Bland, Larry I. and Sharon R. Ritenour, eds. *The Papers of George Catlett Marshall.* 2 Volumes. Baltimore, MD: Johns Hopkins University Press, 1981, 194.

179 Mark Stoler. *George C. Marshall: Soldier-Statesman of the American Century.* Boston: Twayne Publishers, 1989, 46.

180 Bland, 194.

181 Ambrose, *Eisenhower, Soldier and President,* 40.

182 *George C. Marshall Papers,* Vol. I, 259.

183 *George C. Marshall Papers,* Vol. I, letter dated April 25, 1934.

184 Ibid.

185 Bland, 626.

186 Brandon, 123.

187 Puryear, *Nineteen Stars,* 162-163.

188 Brandon, 112.

189 Ibid., 122.

190 Ibid., 116.

191 Ibid., 123.

192 Eisenhower, *General Ike,* 6-7.

193 Letter on file at Eisenhower Library

194 Eisenhower, *General Ike,* 7.

195 David, *Ike and Mamie,* 89.

196 Susan Eisenhower. *Mrs. Ike,* Capital Books, 2002, 76.

197 Brandon, 126.

198 Susan Eisenhower, 77.

199 David, 89.

200 Brandon, 130.

201 Ibid., 135.

202 Ibid., 132.

203 Ibid., 144.

204 Susan Eisenhower, 81.

205 Coffman, *The Regulars,* 178.

206 Ambrose, *Eisenhower, Soldier and President,* 40.

207 Ambrose, *The Supreme Commander,* 7.

208 Ibid., 56.

209 Ambrose, *Eisenhower, Soldier and President,* 40.

210 Puryear, 163.

211 Ambrose, *Eisenhower, Soldier and President,* 42.

212 Letter on file at Eisenhower Library.

213 *Eisenhower Papers,* Johns Hopkins, vol I, 369.

214 Letter on file at Eisenhower Library.

215 Ambrose, *Eisenhower.* Vol 1, 73.

216 Virginia Conner, 50.

217 Blumenson, 349.

218 Ibid., 403.

219 Ibid., 429.

220 D'Este, 202-204.

221 Blumenson, 820-821.

222 Aldrich, 16.

223 Blumenson, 837.

224 Eisenhower, *General Ike,* 11.

225 Bland, 428 and Aldrich, 15.

226 Virginia Conner, 153.

227 *New York Times,* May 2, 1927, 23.

228 AOG Register 1990.

229 Bland, 428.

230 Ibid., 614.

231 Coffman, *The War to End All Wars,* 267.

232 Eisenhower, General Ike, 11.

About the Author

Edward Cox is a major in the U.S. Army. He is currently an assistant professor of American Politics, Public Policy and Strategy in the Department of Social Sciences at the U.S. Military Academy, West Point, NY. He has served in various command and staff positions in combat units for twelve years, including two years in Iraq. He holds a bachelor's degree in American politics from the U.S. Military Academy and master's degrees in public administration and international relations from Syracuse University.

Made in the USA
Monee, IL
12 September 2020

41864394R00079